MAKERS
of the
MUSLIM
WORLD

Amir Khusraw

SELECTION OF TITLES IN THE MAKERS OF
THE MUSLIM WORLD SERIES

Series editor: Patricia Crone,
Institute for Advanced Study, Princeton

'Abd al-Malik, Chase F. Robinson
Abd al-Rahman III, Maribel Fierro
Abu Nuwas, Philip Kennedy
Ahmad ibn Hanbal, Christopher Melchert
Ahmad Riza Khan Barelwi, Usha Sanyal
Al-Ma'mun, Michael Cooperson
Al-Mutanabbi, Margaret Larkin
Amir Khusraw, Sunil Sharma
El Hajj Beshir Agha, Jane Hathaway
Fazlallah Astarabadi and the Hurufis, Shazad Bashir
Ibn 'Arabi, William C. Chittick
Ibn Fudi, Ahmad Dallal
Ikhwan al-Safa, Godefroid de Callatay
Shaykh Mufid, Tamima Bayhom-Daou

For current information and details of other books in the
series, please visit www.oneworld-publications.com/
makers-of-the-muslim-world

MAKERS
of the
MUSLIM
WORLD

Amir Khusraw
The Poet of Sufis and Sultans

SUNIL SHARMA

ONEWORLD
ACADEMIC

A Oneworld Book

First published by Oneworld Publications, 2005
Reprinted, 2019

ISBN: 978-1-85168-362-8
eISBN: 978-1-78074-191-8

Typeset by Jayvee, Trivandrum, India
Cover and text design by Design Deluxe
Printed and bound in Great Britain by Clays Ltd, Elcograf S.p.A.

Oneworld Publications
10 Bloomsbury Street
London WC1B 3SR
England

MIX
Paper from
responsible sources
FSC
www.fsc.org   FSC® C018072

Don't be proud of your poetry, Khusraw,
    There are many poets, of the past and future.
If you want your words to be faultless,
    Look at them from your enemy's point of view.
Everybody thinks their words are great,
    And a friend will praise them even more.

CONTENTS

ACKNOWLEDGMENTS

I would like to acknowledge my gratitude to: Professor Heshmat Moayyad with whom I first read Amir Khusraw's poetry; Professor Shafi'i Kadkani who offered many helpful suggestions regarding new directions on this topic; Professor Muzaffar Alam who is always generous with his expertise; and Dr Françoise 'Nalini' Delvoye, who introduced me to the living world of Amir Khusraw in Delhi and beyond.

My friends Shahab Ahmed, Ali Asani, Amanda Hamilton, Qamar-ul Huda, Syed Akbar Hyder, Paul Losensky, Lata Parwani, Alka Patel, and Gregory White have engaged me in stimulating discussions, provided materials, and been encouraging regarding this work.

Thanks are also due to Professor Patricia Crone for commissioning this book and for timely feedback, and to Oneworld Publications for their support.

Pictures: page 25, Arthur M. Sackler Gallery, Smithsonian Institution, Washington, DC – Smithsonian Unrestricted Trust Funds, Smithsonian Collections Acquisition Program and Dr. Arthur M. Sackler; page 30, National Museum, New Delhi; page 49, Courtesy of the Arthur M. Sackler Museum, Harvard University Art Museums, Promised Gift of Stuart Cary Welch, Jr.; pages 55 and 127, Freer Gallery of Art, Smithsonian Institution, Washington, DC.

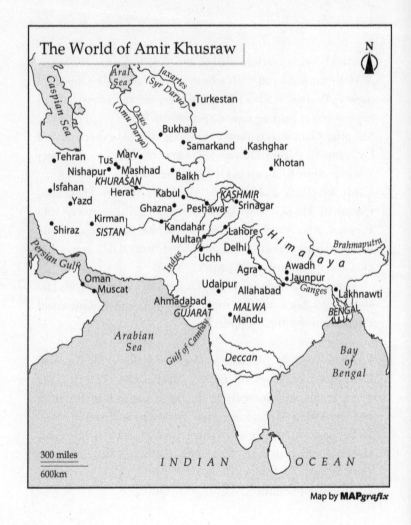

The World of Amir Khusraw

N

Caspian Sea
Aral Sea
Jaxartes (Syr Darya)
Oxus (Amu Darya)
Turkestan
Bukhara
Samarkand
Kashghar
Khotan
Tehran
Tus
Marv
Nishapur
Mashhad
Balkh
KHURASAN
Isfahan
Herat
Kabul
KASHMIR
Yazd
Ghazna
Peshawar
Srinagar
Kirman
Kandahar
Lahore
SISTAN
Shiraz
Multan
Himalaya
Brahmaputra
Indus
Uchh
Delhi
Persian Gulf
Agra
Awadh
Jaunpur
Oman
Muscat
Udaipur
Allahabad
Ganges
Lakhnawti
Ahmadabad
MALWA
GUJARAT
Mandu
BENGAL
Arabian Sea
Gulf of Cambay
Deccan
Bay of Bengal
300 miles
600km
INDIAN   OCEAN

Map by **MAP**grafix

INTRODUCTION

In the collective cultural memory of South Asians, Amir
Khusraw (1253–1325) is the "parrot of India" because he is
considered the greatest Indian poet writing in the Persian
language, which was the *lingua franca* of the eastern Islamic
world in pre-modern times. For a more specialized group of
scholars acquainted with the history of Indian Sufism, he is
also the "Turk of India," a sobriquet bestowed on him by his
spiritual master for his steadfast devotion to Islam. For almost
seven hundred years now, Amir Khusraw (also written as
Khursau or Khusro) has maintained his position as a major
cultural icon in the history of Indian civilization. He is probably
the most popular figure of medieval Indian Islamic culture and
is especially remembered as the founder of Hindustani culture,
which is a synthesis of Muslim and Hindu elements. He helped
to give a distinctive character to Indian Islamic cultural traditions through his contributions in the fields of Indian classical
music, Sufism (Islamic mysticism), *qawwali* (South Asian sufi
music), and Persian literature, and by his role in the development of Hindavi, the vernacular language of the Delhi area,
in which both modern Urdu and Hindi have their roots.
As a courtier, sufi, writer, poet, composer, and musician,
he was a personality to whom few figures in history can be
compared.

Amir Khusraw's legacy is immense and far more widespread than many people realize, from the vast corpus of Persian poetry that is read to this day in Iran, Afghanistan, and Tajikistan to the devotional *qawwalis* that are performed and listened to in the world beyond India and Pakistan. Although he is acknowledged as the best Indian poet in Persian, he does not find his due place in the Iranian national literary canon because he was not Iranian. In South Asia, he is revered for his music and mystical contributions, but most people are only familiar with a small portion of his vast corpus of poetry and prose in Persian, or have no access to these works due to the language barrier. This has not been Amir Khusraw's fate alone. The cultural area in which he lived no longer exists. In the thirteenth century the entire area from Anatolia (now Turkey) to India formed a single belt of what are now called Persianate societies. Though the ruling elite of these lands was Turkish, the high cultural language was Persian, along with Arabic. Once Persian ceased to be a language of learning in South Asia some time in the twentieth century, and the Persianate world was broken by the forces of modern nationalism, many poets, including the eleventh-century Mas'ud Sa'd Salman and the nineteenth-century Ghalib, who wrote prodigiously in Persian as well as in Urdu, have suffered a similar fate. However, Amir Khusraw's compositions in the vernacular sufi and folk literature of north India are still part of a living and dynamic tradition.

Yet Amir Khusraw's personality is shrouded in mystery and those who attempt to understand his biography find it hard to reconcile the facts of his life: How could he have been a courtier and a sufi at the same time? How could all the works that are commonly attributed to him be authentic? Did he really write poetry in Hindavi and invent so many musical instruments? These questions are justified to a large extent because although there is quite a bit of autobiographical information in Amir

Khusraw's own writings, and numerous poetic and sufi bio-graphical traditions about him exist from throughout the medieval period, the information is not always reliable and the resulting picture of the poet either remains one-dimensional or appears larger than life.

However, getting to the "real" Amir Khusraw provides many challenges, in the form of sorting through an overwhelming number and variety of original sources and unraveling the lay-ers of cultural myth and legend that his personality has been draped with over the centuries. There are all kinds of hagio-graphical and biographical traditions about Amir Khusraw in the form of apocryphal anecdotes about his life, especially con-nected with his relationships to his friend, the poet-sufi Hasan Sijzi, and their spiritual master, Nizamuddin Awliya, which though invaluable for the history of the poet's reception in the popular imagination tend to obfuscate what we can glean directly from the poet's own writings and those of his contem-poraries. In academic circles, Amir Khusraw is known in three separate fields: to historians of medieval India and Persian literature as a writer of Persian poetry and prose; to ethno-musicologists and Islamists as a mystic whose Persian and Hindavi verses form the core of *qawwali* performance; and to art historians as a skillful story-teller whose quintet of narrative tales *(khamsah)* has a rich illustrated manuscript tradition from all over the Persianate world. How can these three personal-ities be brought together? In trying to present the totality of the life and works of Amir Khusraw a reader is overwhelmed by historical tidbits of information and the large body of the poet's works.

Amir Khusraw's literary achievements form a seminal part of the literary canon, not just of Indo-Persian, but of a univer-sal canon that includes the works of classical poets such as Nizami, Sa'di and Hafiz, and his poetry can help to expand our knowledge about the culture of medieval Persian literature. He also offers us access to the culture and history of pre-Mughal north India, which though the object of study in a thriving academic discipline is sometimes viewed by non-experts as an age of nothing but conquest and conversion, devoid of artistic and humanistic achievements. This was actually a formative period for the establishment of the institutions of Indian Islam and the genesis of various Indian cultural traditions that endure to our day. Perhaps this age of Indian history appears less grand to us today because the earliest rulers of Delhi, the Ilbarids, the Khaljis, and the Tughlaqs, were not celebrated in the accounts of European travelers as were the Mughals, and because the material remains from this time are not as numerous. However, it is useful to bear in mind that the Mughals, the rulers of the Deccan and other regional kingdoms in India, continued political and cultural institutions set up much earlier, albeit with new strains of influence from other sources. There is no doubt that Amir Khusraw with his involvement in the court of Delhi and in the local sufi order, both centers of power that affected the lives of ordinary people in the thirteenth and fourteenth centuries, is a key figure in understanding the complexities of the social and political order of that time.

The present work is an attempt to present Amir Khusraw in the context of the society he lived in, which was complex and unique in many respects, rooted in local traditions but also remarkably cosmopolitan because of the use of Persian in courtly and literary circles. However, he is not just part of the South Asian past. In our time, the figure of Amir Khusraw takes on a particular relevance due to the volatile political and communal situation in South Asia. Contesting views exist today on the definition of "Indian" culture and who are the rightful heirs to the medieval past. Another arena for this conflict is the linguistic one of the modern languages Hindi and Urdu, which have shared origins in Amir Khusraw's Hindavi but have drifted apart culturally. It is hoped that an introduction such as this one will prove to be useful to students as well as to specialists in the field. Despite the problems involved in translating pre-modern poetry and prose, translations of some original texts in the appendices, one a biographical account of Amir Khusraw by one of his contemporaries and the other a translation of one of his tales, are provided to bring the reader one step closer to the world of Amir Khusraw. All translations are the author's except where otherwise indicated.

2

IN A CITY OF SULTANS, SUFIS, AND POETS: AMIR KHUSRAW AND DELHI

MUSLIM INDIA IN THE THIRTEENTH CENTURY

Communities of Muslims were already established in India in the early years of Islam, primarily in western India, on the Malabar coast, and in the regions of Sindh and Gujarat, but it was the conquest of northern India by Sultan Mahmud (d. 1030), the ruler of a vast empire, that brought about the inclusion of India in the world of Islam. The Ghaznavids were Turks based in Ghazni (in present-day Afghanistan) and they were the cultural and political heirs of the Persian Samanid dynasty based in Bukhara (in present-day Uzbekistan). The Samanids had established themselves in the early ninth century and their institutions and courtly culture had a Persian orientation, as was true of the eastern Islamic world in general. As the Turks of Central Asia were converted to Islam and served as slaves in the courts and armies of the Muslim rulers, they in turn became empowered and began new dynasties. The Ghaznavids and Seljuqs were two such ruling houses in this period, and the institution of rulers of slave origins continued in Delhi.

By the later part of the eleventh century, the rule of the Ghaznavids had been established in northwestern India, with the frontier city of Lahore becoming a thriving cultural center. At this time, the city was home to court poets such as Abu al-Faraj Runi (d. c. 1102) and Mas'ud Sa'd Salman (d. 1121), and the sufi al-Hujviri "Data Ganj Bakhsh" (d. 1071), who wrote the first Persian sufi manual, *Kashf al-mahjub* (Unveiling of the Veiled) and whose shrine in Lahore is a center for mystics and pilgrims to this day. The Ghaznavids increasingly turned eastwards as they lost their Iranian possessions to another Turkish dynasty, the Seljuqs, but even in the east they eventually lost out to a ruling house known as the Ghurids, based in Ghur, in the hilly regions of western Afghanistan. As successors to the Ghaznavids, the Ghurids shifted the centers of power and culture closer to the Indian heartlands and away from the frontier, to the cities of Uch, Multan, and Delhi.

At the same time that Muslims were reaching the Bengal frontier, in 1192, at the battle of Tarain under the leadership of Mu'inuddin Muhammad, the Ghurids won a decisive victory over the Hindu rulers, the Chauhans, and the Turkish slave Qutbuddin Aybek was appointed as deputy in Delhi, which became the seat of a new polity. In the next few decades, Muslims began to consolidate their power under the rule of sultans such as Iltutmish (r. 1211–36), who was succeeded by his formidable daughter, Raziya (r. 1236–40), one of the few women rulers in the Islam world, Nasiruddin (r. 1246–66), and Balban (r. 1266–87). These rulers of slave origins were followed by the Khalji and Tughlaq dynasties whose rule lasted until the fourteenth century.

Meanwhile, the Mongol foray into Central Asia and Iran in the early thirteenth century had set forth a large wave of migration: many scholars, poets, artisans, and religious figures left for India and settled in and around Delhi, which as a place of refuge had come to be known as the Dome of Islam (*qubbat al-Islam*). These émigrés brought with them their skills, institutions, and religious and literary traditions, which came into contact with local cultural practices, thus resulting in the flowering of a uniquely Indian form of Islamic civilization. The Delhi of that time was not the Delhi of today: even old Delhi is largely a Mughal construction and remains so in popular imagination. Rather, the thirteenth-century city was an amalgamation of several cities whose traces have not completely disappeared from the topography of the land. The foundations of this city were laid near the Hindu citadel of Lalkot, in the present-day area of Mehrauli, and soon the villages of Kilokhri, Siri (modern-day Shahpur), Ghiyaspur, and Jahanpanah all formed part of this thriving metropolis. The architectural monuments built over the course of the thirteenth and fourteenth centuries, such as the tombs of the early rulers, the victory tower Qutb Minar, the Qubbat al-Islam mosque, the water reservoirs Hawz-i Shamsi and the Hawz-i Khass, the city of Tughlaqabad, attest to the existence of a powerful and centralized ruling house that was conscious of its unique position in the world of Islam and in South Asia.

By the time of Amir Khusraw's birth in 1253, in half a century under a succession of Turkish rulers, Delhi had become a cosmopolitan city renowned throughout the Islamic world for its institutions of learning and as a haven for wandering scholars and poets. In the early days of the slave rulers, the city was administered by an elite corps of Turkish nobles known as the *chihilgan* (the Forty) whose power declined over time as Indians began to participate in the government. The indigenous population consisted chiefly of Hindus, Jains, and two broad categories of Muslims: Indian converts and immigrants from Central Asia who had settled there as refugees or were simply drawn by the centers of learning, such as the Mu'izzi *madrasah*, and by the generous patronage of the rulers. Sufis also passed through the city, as did merchants since it was also a flourishing commercial center. The Moroccan traveler Ibn Battuta reached Delhi in 1333, a few years after Amir Khusraw's death, and describes the society in great detail. According to Ibn Battuta, "Dihli [Delhi], the metropolis of India, is a vast and magnificent city, uniting beauty with strength. It is surrounded by a wall that has no equal in the world, and is the largest city in India, nay in the entire Muslim Orient" (Ibn Battuta, 1957: 194). A contemporary source, the historian Ziyauddin Barni (d. fourteenth century), states that the presence of so many luminaries, among whom was the sufi master Nizamuddin Awliya and others, had made Delhi the envy of Baghdad and Cairo, and the equal of Constantinople and Jerusalem!

A description of the entry of Qutbuddin Aybek into the city of Delhi from an early historical source, Hasan Nizami's *Taj al-ma'asir*, conveys the pomp and grandeur of the military court in the usual hyperbolic style of the time:

> Men of letters and soldiers along with attendants and servants of all categories presented themselves at the court and discharged the obligation of showering encomiums and offering prayers for the king. The city and its suburbs appeared fresh and adorned like the garden of paradise. Its doors and walls were embellished with the brocade of Rum and gold cloth of China. They made elegant domes from the top of which even a fast flying bird could not pass, and the height of which could not be measured by the engineer of thought and mind. Its battlements were so high that they [touched] the circle of blue heaven, in fact, they rose beyond the pinnacle of the silver coated palaces and the golden court (sky).
>
> The brightness of the flash of swords and other arms that were hanging about that place dissolved the sense of vision

and the glare of their reflection was as dazzling to the eyes as
the sun. They shone like a casket full of gems and the zodiacal
sign with all its stars. Or you would say that luminous
heavenly bodies had descended on the earth, or maybe
dark substances had acquired the gloss of pure gems.
(Hasan Nizami, 1998: 135)

Despite achieving such a status within a short time, throughout
the thirteenth century the capital city of the Sultanate was
beset with political upheavals and instability, on the one hand
due to the repeated Mongol raids in the northwest, sometimes
right into the environs of Delhi, and on the other to the ruthless
battles of succession for the throne and the short-lived and
unstable rule of usurpers. Nevertheless, there were prolonged
periods of stability during which many artistic and cultural
endeavors were undertaken and creative energies were
allowed to flower, as witnessed by the architectural and literary
monuments that survive from this period.

Arabic was the language of the religious sciences and technical disciplines, while Persian was more widely used, both in its
written and spoken form. It was the literary and cultural language of the eastern Islamic world and the literature written in
it circulated in a large cosmopolitan literary world often
described as Persianate, which extended from Anatolia and the
Caucasus to Bengal at this time. The Samanids and Ghaznavids
had been the earliest patrons of Persian court literature, and
even though the Ghaznavid sultan Mahmud and some of the
Muslim rulers of India were of Turkish origin, Turkish never
became a literary language in India nor did it receive courtly
patronage. Hindavi was the language of the people around
Delhi, but being in a formative stage, it still had not achieved
high cultural status. The impetus to its development into a full-
fledged literary medium was given by the sufis, who had more
direct contact with the populace.

In the history of the spread of Islam in the Indian subcontinent, the role of the sufis cannot be overestimated. It was due
to the tireless efforts of these mystics, who wandered off into
every corner of the land and made contacts with people at all
levels, that Islam became part of the local religious landscape.
It was also due to the medieval sufis and Hindu mystics that vernacular languages came into their own and took their place
next to the more prestigious languages of India, Persian and
Sanskrit. There were two primary sufi orders (*silsilah*) in India
at this time, and they varied fundamentally in their practices
and their relationship to the state as well as to the populace.
Originating in Iraq, the Suhrawardiyah sufi order was established in the thirteenth century in Multan, on the western frontier of the Delhi Sultanate, by Shaykh Bahauddin Zakariya, at
about the same time that the Chishtiyah order became prominent in Delhi, right in the capital city. The Chishti presence in
Delhi dated from the time of the visit of the great master Shaykh
Mu'inuddin Chishti who came there in 1193 but moved on to
Ajmer (Rajasthan) in the heart of the Hindu dominions, and
from that of his disciple Qutbuddin Bakhtiyar Kaki who had
settled in Delhi, where his tomb is situated. The towering figure
among them and the most influential *pir* was Nizamuddin
Awliya (d. 1325), who had inherited the leadership (*khilafat*) of
the order from Shaykh Fariduddin in 1266.

No study of the social or literary history of the times can
ignore the presence of Nizamuddin Awliya in the city and his
influence on the lives of so many people of his time. By all
accounts, he had a charismatic personality and led a life stead-
fastly devoted to providing for the spiritual needs of his community. Although the Chishtis preferred to have nothing to do
with the sultan and his court in Delhi, the power they had over
the populace created tensions between them and the sultan on
the one hand, and between the sufis and the religious clergy

('*ulama*), who were not favorably disposed to them either, on the other. The Suhrawardis maintained friendly relations with the Delhi sultans for the most part and, unlike the Chishtis, belonged to an affluent and land-owning institution. In contrast, the Chishtis did not accept any grants from the sultans and emphasized poverty and austerity, and as a result they exerted an abiding spiritual power over the hearts of the people of Delhi. Generous throughout his lifetime, Nizamuddin Awliya, who never married, is said to have given away all his belongings before he died.

EARLY LIFE AND CAREER

Amir Khusraw's life is inextricably linked with the political and social history of Delhi. In his lifetime, he served many noblemen and rulers, traveled across the expanse of South Asia in their service, and remained attached to the Chishti sufis of Delhi. He provides many autobiographical details about himself in his writings, but most of the information is incidental and mainly concerned with the development of his poetic sensibilities from childhood to maturity. Some of the biographical details accepted as historical truth today, especially those connected with his family's origins and his father, are actually found for the first time only in later sources that date several centuries after the poet's lifetime and cannot be taken at face value. Scholarship in our time has contributed to a better knowledge about the poet's early life than had been available through the intervening centuries.

Amir Khusraw's father was Sayfuddin Shamsi, whose Turkish name was Lachin, perhaps named after the obscure Lachin tribe from Transoxiana in Central Asia. He may have been of slave origins and named after his first master. He served Sultan

Iltutmish (r. 1211–36) in the police force of the city. In a contemporary chronicle, the *Tabaqat-i Nasiri*, the author Minhaj-i Siraj Juzjani provides a biographical sketch of one of the slaves of Sultan Iltutmish who can plausibly be identified as Amir Khusraw's father:

> Early on in his life, he was taken from the Qipchaq tribes and his native country and enslaved. He fell into the service of the generous Khvajah Shamsuddin 'Ajami, who was the Chief of the Merchants of the countries of Iran, Iraq, Khvarazm, and Ghazni. Even until this time he is called after that great man. When the sultan bought him and he entered the service of the lofty court of Shamsuddin Iltutmish, he achieved a high rank.

Although the poet himself does not mention these facts, it was a common practice for Turkish slaves to attain high positions at the courts of Iranian rulers. Over time, as Amir Khusraw's prestige and fame as a mystic increased, writers of his biography wove more than a few variant and creative accounts about the origins of his family.

Sayfuddin Shamsi married the daughter of 'Imad al-Mulk, an Indian Muslim who was also in the service of the sultan, as the keeper first of the royal falcon and later of the royal horse. Although first- and second-generation Turkish immigrants were generally an elite group who looked down upon the recently converted Indian Muslims, it appears that intermarriage did take place between the two communities. Amir Khusraw was proud of both sides of his lineage, and his life and writings symbolize a synthesis of the two different cultures that encountered each other in this land. He appropriately calls himself an Indian Turk (in India the word came to be synonymous with "Muslim") and his sufi master called him the "Turk of God."

Sayfuddin Shamsi had three sons, and our poet Abu al-Hasan "Khusraw" was born in 1253 in Delhi and was most certainly the second of the male offspring. His brother 'Izzuddin 'Ali Shah went on to become a scholar of Arabic and Persian, while the other brother, Husamuddin Qutlugh, became a professional soldier like their father. The report of a later biographer that Amir Khusraw's birthplace was the village of Patiyali, although now accepted as a fact, is not confirmed in the poet's own writings. The poet had spent some years there while serving in the military. There are other claims for his birthplace as well. According to another improbable eighteenth-century biographical account, the poet's birthplace was Balkh, the birthplace of the Persian sufi poet Mawlana Jalaluddin Rumi (d. 1273), and he came to India as a child with his family. In fact, Amir Khusraw's statements about his relationship to the capital city suggest that Delhi was his birthplace.

In an autobiographical statement, the poet describes his father in glowing terms as having an angelic nature but at the same time a regal bearing. Although Sayfuddin was illiterate he wanted his sons to receive a proper education. He died in battle when the poet was eight, and as a result, the boys were raised by their maternal grandfather, a powerful nobleman in service at the court for over eighty years of his life, and by uncles. Amir Khusraw writes with great fondness about his grandfather, who was the most influential figure in his life during his formative years. The three brothers studied with Mawlana Sa'duddin, and even before he reached his teens Amir Khusraw had started to compose poetry. His talent did not go unnoticed by those around him, and in the introduction to his first collection of poems, he describes how he was put to the test at an early age:

One morning the city magistrate Khvajah Asil sent for my teacher Khvajah Sa'duddin to have a letter composed by him. I went with him taking along my pen-case. In the house of that

gentleman Khvajah 'Izzuddin was an employee and he was
knowledgeable about writing poetry. There was a notebook
open beside him into which he would plunge like a diver,
extract gem-like verses and recite them. My teacher said to
him: "This young boy who is my pupil is serious about poetry.
Give him the notebook and let us observe how he reads."
Khvajah 'Izzuddin gave the notebook to me and I began to
read aloud. I recited each verse in harmonious tones such that
everyone became teary-eyed and there was amazement on all
sides. My teacher said, "The recitation of verses is easy. He
should be tested with the composition of verses so that his
natural brilliance may shine like a mirror." Khvajah 'Izzuddin
tested me with four unrelated things: hair, egg, arrow, and
melon. In the presence of everyone in the assembly, I recited
the following couplets:

> Every strand of hair in the curly tresses of that beauty
> Has attracted a thousand grains [eggs] of amber.
> Know her heart to be as straight as an arrow,
> For like the melon the choice part is found inside.

As soon as I recited this quatrain, the Khvajah complimented
me abundantly and asked me my name. I said it was Khusraw.
Then he asked me my father's name. I said it was Sultani
Shamsi. He said, "Since a coin (*sultani*) is connected with royalty, you will be called Sultani."

This was how the poet got his first pen name (*takhallus*), which
he used in his earliest poems. Aptly, both "Sultani" and
"Khusraw" have regal connotations and the poet was always
affiliated with royalty.

It was at his grandfather's house that Amir Khusraw met
Nizamuddin Awliya, at this time a young mystic who had just
moved to Delhi for his education, and who would later become
one of the most powerful men of the city and the most important person in the poet's life. The other intimate person in Amir

Khusraw's life was the court poet and fellow sufi, Hasan Sijzi (d. 1337). Hasan was the same age as Khusraw and both were honored with the title of *Amir* for their prowess in the art of poetry. Their lives revolved around the same institutions and personalities, but Hasan's poetry has not received its just recognition in our time, although Nizamuddin Awliya has been immortalized in history by his writings. The depth and intensity of the friendship between Hasan and Amir Khusraw gave rise to many fanciful accounts about the nature of their relationship, including some that claim they were lovers. The biographical traditions and anecdotes about personal details in Persian texts should not be taken at face value, and it is necessary to examine the background and historical context of the author introducing facts and stories that usually appear only centuries later. Whatever the truth may have been, their shared love of poetry and devotion to their *pir* allowed for a deep bond to be forged between Amir Khusraw and Hasan that lasted throughout their lives. The senior poet Shihab Mahmira, who was active at the Delhi court, was a mentor to Amir Khusraw and probably helped him to get started as a professional poet, a career that took off seriously when the poet was twenty and when his grandfather passed away at the age of one hundred and thirteen years.

From 1277 until his death in 1325, Amir Khusraw was a courtier and poet, first in the service of princes and nobles, then at the court of the sultan of Delhi. Serving five rulers and witnessing the rule of several more, he managed to survive the political intrigues of the various factions and individuals at work in Delhi. This probably propelled him further into the world of the sufis that seldom overlapped with the political world of the ruler and courtiers, and he remained a link between the two. A ruler would often be arbitrary in showing favor to poets and sufis of the city, and judging by the lives of many medieval Persian poets, the perils of being a panegyrist at court were great. Court poets and artists were part of a complex network of patronage that started from the royal court, and included different strata of society such as the nobility and even the bourgeois classes. The professional poet is often regarded as a sycophant and mercenary because he shifted allegiances without qualms, but he was simply performing his job. In this short topical poem, the poet reveals his view of his profession:

> Composing panegyric kills the heart,
> Even if the poetry is fresh and eloquent.
> A lamp is extinguished by a breath,
> Even if it is the breath of Jesus.

The poet admits that praising patrons is a tiresome task even if it results in fine poetry. Jesus' breath, which is supposed to be life-bestowing, cannot prevent the flame of a lamp from being blown out just as good poetry does not completely erase the negative aspects of insincere praise.

Often Amir Khusraw and poets like him state that they utter no lies but only report the truth. But court poets were not objective recorders of the character and deeds of their patrons, rather they were professionals whose skills were valued according to certain factors in the market such as current literary trends and the existence of generous patrons. There was also a whole class of wandering poets who were continuously seeking better prospects for themselves. Once a poet became successful and a favorite at court, he could not easily dissociate himself from his patron. The court poet was not just a boon companion (*nadim*) and friend to a ruler or prince, he also was an advisor who could use his poetry as a mirror for setting ideals of ethical behavior. Amir Khusraw often appears to walk a thin line between sincerity and sycophancy, but exonerates

himself by including a moral and didactic subtext while praising patrons who were hardly paragons of virtue.

The art and practice of poetry had a respected and requisite
function in Persianate courtly culture. In the *Fava'id al-fu'ad*
(Morals of the Heart), a record of the discourses of
Nizamuddin Awliya by the poet Hasan, it is reported that the
sufi told the following story:

> Once, Sultan Shams ad-din was holding court when the poet
> Nasiri arrived and offered a poem in his praise that began:
>
> > O you, from fear of whose might strife itself seeks refuge,
> > Your sword exacts from infidels wealth and elephants huge.
>
> The Sultan, while listening to this poem, was also busy with
> other matters, and Nasiri continued to recite some more
> verses. The Sultan at last turned his mind to poetry.
> Addressing Nasiri, he asked:
>
> > "O you, from fear of whose might strife itself seeks refuge,
> > Your sword exacts from infidels wealth and elephants huge –
>
> Would you please recite the verses that came after this?"
> Commented the master, "Look how sharp was his memory;
> even while occupied with other matters, he could still recall
> the opening the verses of this poem!" (Hasan Sijzi, 1992: 319)

This anecdote illustrates the attention to poetry that a proper
ruler ought to display. Poetry served as a medium for commun-
icating with the world at large and also for conferring cultural
legitimacy on a court by forging connections to the past. A
court poet was the spokesman for a ruler and the ideals he
wished to espouse. The relation between patron and poet was a
delicate one; the former demanded complete loyalty while the
latter expected suitable monetary compensation and apprecia-
tion for his poems.

Amir Khusraw's first patron was Kishlu Khan (also known as
Malik Chhajju), a nobleman and nephew of the sultan, Balban

(r. 1266–87). For his debut at court, the poet wrote an inaugural poem in praise of his new patron, appropriately using the rhyme word "appeared" (*numud*):

> The sun was invisible when morning
> Appeared in the company of the scented breeze.
> I asked the morning, "Where is your sun?"
> Heaven made the face of Malik Chhajju appear.

Persian court poets normally used a highly metaphorical language to describe their patrons in panegyric poems (*qasidah*). Such poems were more formal and difficult than love lyrics (*ghazals*). Though clearly hyperbolic, they were often infused with genuine feeling, for the bond between patron and poet was sometimes very strong and, as mentioned above, poets at court often had the additional role of boon companion. With many of his patrons, Amir Khusraw was not just a professional poet but also a friend and associate. Based in Sunnam, west of Delhi, Malik Chhajju was celebrated as a generous patron of poets. However, at the end of two years' service, Amir Khusraw fell out of favor when he accepted a gift from his patron's cousin, the emperor's son Bughra Khan, who was also a great admirer of his poems.

As a result, Amir Khusraw took up service with his new patron and settled in Samana (Panjab), but he only stayed there for a short time before moving on to Lakhnawti (Bengal) where Bughra Khan was sent to quell a rebellion. Bughra Khan was a connoisseur of music and the arts, but the poet soon left his service and returned to Delhi because he missed the city and his family. He often speaks candidly of his deep attachment to the city, especially since his family and friends were there. In one of his poems written when he was absent from Delhi he says:

> My home was the Dome of Islam,
> It was the *qiblah* for kings of the seven climes.

Delhi is the twin of pure paradise,
A prototype of the heavenly throne on an earthly scroll.

These encomiastic references to Delhi also suggest that this was indeed the city of his birth. Such statements of his helped in building the reputation of the Sultanate capital as a major center of Persian poetry in the eastern Islamic world, where his name came to be linked with that of his city. Therefore, he is often given the added appellation of Dihlavi, of Delhi.

In 1280, Amir Khusraw attracted the attention and became the *nadim* of the young prince Khan Malik Sultan Muhammad who was a Maecenas of his time and by all accounts a warm, generous, and charming individual. Prince Muhammad's court at Multan was a significant cultural center that for a time rivaled even Delhi. The prince was fond of poetry and gathered the best poets around him. Multan was home to the Suhrawardiyah order, and Amir Khusraw must have had contacts with the sufis based there. He most certainly witnessed and participated in devotional performances of singing sessions that would later develop into the *qawwali*. The memory of the famous Persian mystical poet Fakhruddin 'Iraqi (d. 1289), who had lived in Multan for twenty-five years before returning to the western Islamic lands, must have been fresh in the community, and Amir Khusraw must have heard 'Iraqi's *ghazals* which were popular with the Chishti sufis. Hasan had also accompanied Amir Khusraw to Multan in the service of Prince Muhammad. It is reported that Muhammad twice invited the famous poet of Iran, Sa'di (d. 1292) of Shiraz, a literary giant and model for all poets writing in Persian at this time, to come and settle in Multan where he was going to name an institution of learning after him. It is even claimed that Sa'di did visit India to meet Amir Khusraw but these accounts are not confirmed by any historical or poetic source of the period.

Amir Khusraw's sojourn in Multan lasted five years and came to an abrupt end in 1285 when Timur Khan Tatar led a Mongol foray into the Panjab. In the ensuing battle, Prince Muhammad was killed and Amir Khusraw taken captive. The poet spent a short time as a prisoner, a horrifying experience that he described later in graphic detail. He and Hasan both wrote moving elegies on the death of their beloved patron, and when they returned home, all of Delhi was in mourning for the prince who was henceforth called the Martyr Prince (*Sultan-i shahid*). The powerful elegy by Amir Khusraw in eleven stanzas begins:

> Is this an earthly occurrence or has a calamity appeared from
> the sky?
> Is this a disaster or has the day of resurrection appeared in
> the world?
> The flood of iniquity has reached the foundations of the world
> Through the crack that appeared in Hindustan this year.
> The assembly of friends is scattered like flower petals by
> the wine,
> It seems that autumn has appeared in the garden.
> Deprived of seeing him, every eyelash is like a spear in
> the eye,
> Blood has come forth from every spearhead.
> Hearts are constricted since the world has fallen apart,
> Pearls are falling since the string has been broken.
> People shed so many tears in all directions
> That five other rivers have appeared in Multan.
> I wanted to speak from the fire in my heart
> But a hundred fiery tongues appeared in my mouth.
> The death of the prince has turned the whole world upside
> down.

Written in the typical poetic idiom of the time, the poem is a poignant and sincere elegy for the virtuous young patron, and it is said that when the sultan in Delhi heard the poem he was moved to tears. The set of questions in the beginning of the poem and its intensely emotional tone allow the listener to share in the poet's grief. For his part, Hasan wrote his elegy in prose, in order not to be compared with and compete with his friend.

After returning to Delhi, Amir Khusraw kept a low profile, spending time with his family; he was especially close to his mother. The political situation in the capital city was not stable at this time and he went east to Avadh for a brief stint in the service of the new governor, the freedman 'Ali Sarjandar Hatim Khan. In 1289, on a visit to Delhi, Amir Khusraw was summoned by the sultan, Kayqubad (r. 1287–90), and commissioned to write a poem in commemoration of the reunion between the sultan and his father Bughra Khan, the erstwhile patron of the poet. This work, entitled *Qiran al-sa'dayn* (Conjunction of Two Stars), was the first narrative poem on a theme from the history of his own time, and an innovative step in his growth as a court poet, as will be discussed below. Sultan Kayqubad did not survive long and died the following year at the age of twenty-two. In this work the poet writes about Delhi:

> Delhi is the refuge of religion and justice,
> It is a paradise of justice – may it endure!
> Since it has the essential qualities of a heavenly garden,
> May God keep it free from troubles.

He goes on to describe the Friday mosque and other buildings in the city, ending this section of the poem with a paean to the young lads of the city:

> O Delhi and its artless idols,
> Who wear turbans and crooked beards.
> They drink the blood of lovers openly,
> Although they drink wine secretly.

> They do not obey commands because
> They are made willful by their extreme beauty.
> Muslims have become sun-worshippers
> Due to these saucy and innocent Hindus.
> These pure Hindu boys
> Have caused me to go to ruin and to drink.
> Ensnared in their curly tresses,
> Khusraw is like a dog with a collar.

Describing its beautiful inhabitants in this playful way was an established mode of praising a city, and ultimately its ruler. The seemingly blasphemous imagery employed here, and the homoerotic element, are also typical of Persian poetry and do not necessarily represent a reality. This was a highly coded language in which poets communicated with their audience and with each other.

One year later, Amir Khusraw joined the court of the new sultan, Jalaluddin Khalji (r. 1290–6), and from then until his death he was connected with the court of Delhi, having progressed from serving provincial officials to being the chief poet at the imperial court. In 1291 the poet wrote the second of his narrative poems on a contemporary subject, *Miftah al-futuh* (Key to Victories), an epic-like work that describes four successful campaigns of Jalaluddin Khalji against the rebellious Malik Chhajju, who had been the first patron of Amir Khusraw, the rajas of Avadh and Jhayin, and the Mongols. Under this sultan, and his nephew and successor, 'Alauddin Khalji (r. 1296–1316), who were of Afghan background, Amir Khusraw was at his peak as a professional poet. Although the arts, and especially Persian literature, received generous patronage from the various sultans of Delhi throughout the poet's life, the reign of 'Alauddin Khalji witnessed a cultural renaissance that would not be seen again until almost three centuries later under the Mughals. In an unusual choice for him, Amir

Amir Khusraw presents a poem to Sultan 'Alauddin.

Khusraw described the military exploits of this patron in a prose work, *Khaza'in al-futuh* (Treasures of Victories), written in 1309. As a result of the patronage of this sultan, architecture and building activities flourished and all sorts of historical, poetic, and scientific works were written in Persian. Delhi was at the apex of its glory in these years and the career of its greatest poet was at its height.

When Jalaluddin Khalji became sultan, he was a man of advanced years, but he had a great zeal for the arts and was an ardent admirer of Amir Khusraw's poetry. The historian Ziyauddin Barni, a younger contemporary of the poet, paints a vivid portrait of the monarch:

> Sultan Jalaluddin was a connoisseur and patron of the arts. He had an elegant disposition and could compose quatrains and *ghazals*. What clearer proof could there have been of his refined nature and connoisseurship [than] that just at the time when Sultan Jalaluddin had become the war minister he extolled Amir Khusraw, who was the chief of the court poets from first to last, and held him in great esteem ... and fixed upon him a stipend of 1200 *tanka*s which had been his father's, and gave him horses, vestments, and his own slaves. When he became king, Amir Khusraw became one of his intimates at court and served as keeper of the Qur'an ... It was due to the refinement of Sultan Jalaluddin that the pleasure assemblies were arrayed with such matchless friends, peerless boon companions, slender cupbearers, fair beauties, and pleasing minstrels that could only be seen in paradise.

Barni goes on to describe the sultan's courtly gatherings with his boon companions who were his associates in battle and banquet (*razm va bazm*), chief among whom was the poet Amir Khusraw. The other boon companions were Tajuddin 'Iraqi, Mu'ayyad Jajarmi, and Mu'ayyad Divanah. There was a great deal of drinking, jesting, and witty exchange of words at these assemblies,

accompanied by music, singing, and dancing. Among the enter-
tainers, the *ghazal* singers were Sultan Amir Khassah and Hamid
Rajah. Barni adds that "Amir Khusraw would bring new *ghazals*
daily to those assemblies and the sultan became enamored of his
poems and rewarded him handsomely." The cupbearers (*saqis*)
of the assembly were the beautiful and coquettish boys Haybat
Khan, Nizam Kharitahdar and Yulduzsar. Among the minstrels
he names Muhammad Sinh Changi (the harpist). There were
even women participants at these parties: Futuha, Naqa'i, and
Nusrat Khatun sang while Nusrat Bibi and Mihrafruz danced.
Barni gets so carried away in describing these convivial gatherings that he declares that they were only the stuff of dreams now.

This fascinating vignette of courtly life is an indication of how
removed this world was from that of the sufis and their assemblies, with the common factor being the poems of Amir
Khusraw which would have been performed in both places. In
this way, the poet forms a link between the two milieus for the
production and performance of poetry and music of his time,
the royal and the sufi courts, and blurs the distinctions between
the two modes of poetic expression.

The poet's third historical narrative poem, *'Ashiqah*
(Beloved), completed in 1315, was written after he had fin-
ished his quintet of narrative poems (*khamsah*) during the early
years of 'Alauddin Khalji's reign and is probably his best-known
work. The theme of this poem is as fabulous as any fiction,
describing the tragic love of the young prince Khizr Khan for
Devaldi, a Hindu princess of Gujarat.

KEEPING COMPANY WITH SUFIS

The sufi literary scene of Amir Khusraw's time was as brisk as
the courtly one. The historian Barni, a close friend of Amir

Khusraw and Hasan, was also affiliated with the Chishti order. There were a number of non-courtly sufi writers such as Ziyauddin Nakhshabi (d. 1350), whose Persian renditions of popular Sanskrit works are the *Tutinamah* (Tales of the Parrot) and the sex manual *Lazzat al-nisa'* (Pleasure of Women). The ecstatic mystic Bu 'Ali Qalandar (d. 1323) had migrated from Iraq and kept company with the Chishtis, and also did not serve at court. Hasan recorded his conversations (in the literary genre of *malfuzat*) with Nizamuddin Awliya on various mystical topics that took place in meetings between 1308 and 1322, in his well-known *Fava'id al-fu'ad*. This work was tremendously popular and influential in later sufi writing of the subcontinent. A similar work about the discourses of the Chishti master, the *Afzal al-fava'id* (Most Excellent Morals), was formerly attributed to Amir Khusraw but this has been established by scholars as spurious.

The *khanaqah* was a thriving alternative space in this society outside the court for the creation and performance of poetry. Amir Khusraw seems to be one of few poets, one can even say the only one in the entire history of pre-modern Persian poetry, who was simultaneously a court poet in the business of praising kings and a sufi poet whose poems were performed in a mystical context. Amir Khurd (d. 1369), a younger contemporary and biographer of the sufis of the Chishtiyah order, writes apologetically about Amir Khusraw being a courtier and sufi at the same time, and states that he was one of those about whom it can be said, "Devote yourself to the service of the sultan and be a sufi" (see Appendix I).

It was precisely in these years that the poet's affiliation with the Chishti sufis was strengthened. By this time, Nizamuddin Awliya had achieved an eminent status in the city, and his meeting place (*khanaqah* or *jama'atkhanah*) in the village of Ghiyaspur (the present-day Nizamuddin area of Delhi) was a spiritual center where people from all walks of life were exposed to a mystical and popular form of Islam. The sufis had a major role in the conversion of Indians to Islam, and their presence in Delhi acted as a stabilizing force against the court of the sultan, for they looked after the spiritual welfare of the community. 'Alauddin Khalji's son, Khizr Khan, who was one of Amir Khusraw's patrons, was also a devoted follower of Nizamuddin Awliya. Although 'Alauddin Khalji himself did not frequent the sufi *khanaqah*s, he was positively inclined towards them, and thus Amir Khusraw dedicated many of his works, in fact all the poems of his *khamsah*, to both his mentors simultaneously.

It is tempting to employ the relationship of the renowned Persian mystic poet Rumi, who had a deep attachment to his spiritual companion, Shams, as a model for understanding the special bond between Amir Khusraw and Nizamuddin Awliya, but one must be careful not to take the comparison too far, and give due credit to the differences in their personalities and historical circumstances. A common point in both relationships is that the two friends complemented each other, as explained by Franklin Lewis: "It is clear that Rumi was more than a simple disciple of Shams; at the same time he was a teacher, one in whom were combined virtues or achievements that Shams himself did not perhaps possess" (Lewis, 2000: 165).

However, there are some remarkable parallels between Amir Khusraw's life and that of Rumi, who lived about a generation before him. As a result of the Mongol incursion into Central Asia, Rumi fled westwards with his family and ended up in Konya, in what is now Turkey. Similarly, a couple of decades later, Amir Khusraw's family moved eastwards and ended up in Delhi, India. Both poets had their origins in the Balkh region in present-day Afghanistan. Amir Khusraw was born in India and identified himself as an Indian, whereas Rumi

was born in Balkh, far from Konya, the city where he was to
settle, and he was ethnically Iranian, whereas Amir Khusraw's
father was Turkish and his mother Indian. They also moved in

Amir Khusraw with Nizamuddin Awliya.

different spheres. In addition, Amir Khusraw was deeply involved in court life, and his Persian writing, whether poetry or prose, is of a panegyric or historical nature. By contrast, Rumi was not a court poet and his output is entirely mystical. Thus, it is appropriate that Khusraw is honoured with the title *Amir* (prince) and Rumi with *Mawlana* (our master).

Most importantly, both were poets of Central Asian origin who deeply influenced the practice of Sufism in their respective parts of the world through their individual emphasis on mystical performance of music and/or dance and the poetic language in which it was expressed. Both were immersed in the local cultures and wrote macaronic poetry, mixing Persian with local languages (Persian, Turkish, Greek, Armenian and Arabic in Rumi's case; Persian and Hindavi in Amir Khusraw's). Since both chose to write their poetry in Persian and authored a large body of *ghazals* on love themes, there are many points of comparison from a literary point of view as well, although one must be sensitive to the different contexts in which they wrote.

Amir Khusraw celebrated his spiritual master, who was known as the *mahbub-i ilahi* (Beloved of God), in poems written in all the literary genres available to him. In the following lines taken from a longer poem, he describes Nizamuddin Awliya with the most sublime images:

> You have the elixir of love in your goblet,
> Your message is the timely word from a beloved.
> The course of union of both worlds
> Is in the space of your two steps.
> You have adorned the path of Farid [Nizamuddin's *pir*],
> That is why your name is Nizam [Adorner].
> The heavens have melted a hundred pure souls
> And inscribed them with your name.
> Your court is the *qiblah* and angels

Fly to your roof like pigeons.
Those who are struggling in pursuit of God,
Find peace in your soothing words.
   The lowly Khusraw will have an eternal life
   Since he has become your slave for a thousand lives.

This is a beautiful description of Nizamuddin Awliya as a spiritual guide of the time, whose court is as grand as that of any ruler. The tender and reverent tone of this poem is a feature of sufi devotional poetry in general. The relationship between poet and *pir* that would last for life is present in all the writings of the poet.

LAST YEARS

Scattered references in Amir Khusraw's works provide a testimony to his deep and sincere attachment to his family. He mentions his maternal grandfather in fond terms as an influential figure in his early years. His mother is also mentioned a few times, and his elegy on her death in 1299, the year in which he also lost one of his two brothers, speaks of his sense of personal loss:

This year two lights departed from my star,
Both my mother and my brother left me.
In one week from my sleeping fortune,
Two fortnightly moons have vanished.
Fate has inflicted two tortures on me,
Heaven reduced me to nothing with two blows.
I mourn twice, two sorrows befell me,
Woe, I suffer two bereavements.
Alas! that one like me was branded twice,
One spark is sufficient to torch a haystack.
One heart cannot carry two aches,

One head cannot endure two hangovers.
Since my mother is under the earth,
If I throw dust over my head, what is there to fear?
O mother of mine, where are you?
Why don't you show me your face?
Come out of the ground laughing,
Take pity on my bitter weeping.
Wherever there is dust from your feet,
It is a reminder for us of paradise.
Your essence was the protection of my life,
It was my succor and support.
When you used to speak,
Your advice was beneficial to me.
Today my lips are sealed
As your silence gives me counsel.

The poet experienced the loss of many dear ones in his life, but this remains one of the most personal elegies he wrote.

As for other family members, there is no mention of his wife anywhere in his works, but there are references to his children. He addresses his daughter Masturah at the end of his work *Matla' al-anvar*, while in his poem *Hasht bihisht*, he gives advice to another daughter, 'Afifah. He gives advice to his son Khizr in *Majnun and Layla*. Two sons, Muhammad and Hajji, died during the poet's lifetime, while another, Malik Ahmad, was known to be active as a court poet under Sultan Firuzshah Tughlaq (r. 1351–75).

In the last decade of his life, Amir Khusraw served the new sultan, Mubarak Shah (r. 1316–20), the young and handsome son of 'Alauddin Khalji, who had come to the throne as the result of a bloody coup. Mubarak Shah was not well-disposed towards Nizamuddin Awliya because his brother Khizr Khan, whom he had killed in his bid for the throne, had been a disciple of the *pir*. This must have been the cause of some tension between him and Amir Khusraw, but since the latter was a senior and established poet by this time he probably was able to maintain a middle ground. During these years, the poet wrote his most unusual work, the narrative poem *Nuh sipihr* (Nine Heavens), the different sections of which are devoted to praising aspects of his patron's life, such as the birth of the young Prince Muhammad, his building activities, and an encomiastic description of India. In this work, which will be discussed below, he declares two reasons for his preference of India: firstly, it is his birthplace, and secondly, it is here that his spiritual master resides.

What followed was a particularly turbulent period of history and it must have taken all of Amir Khusraw's diplomatic skills and spiritual fortitude to maintain a presence at court and celebrate the deeds of his patrons. The promising young monarch Mubarak Shah had become slavishly attached to his male lover, Khusraw Khan, a recent convert to Islam, who eventually usurped the throne after having had Mubarak Shah murdered. A few months later, the usurper was removed by Ghiyasuddin Tughlaq (r. 1320–5). The events of this period have all the drama, debauchery, and violence of ancient Rome in its period of decline, and it was up to the poet to spin all this into an epic. Amir Khusraw's last historical poem, the *Tughlaqnamah*, was written to celebrate the victory of Sultan Ghiyasuddin. The work itself is not remarkable but provides much contemporary historical information on which other sources are silent. Sultan Ghiyasuddin was a pious and orthodox individual who looked askance at the musical gatherings at the *jama'atkhanah* of Nizamuddin Awliya. Amir Khusraw's last patron was Muhammad Shah (r. 1325–51), the son and successor of Ghiyasuddin. The Tughlaq dynasty ruled the Sultanate through the fourteenth century and left an indelible mark on the city of Delhi.

Nizamuddin Awliya passed away in 1325 while Amir Khusraw was with the sultan on a military campaign in the east. It is said that when he heard the news about his *pir*'s death, he recited the following Hindavi couplet that has become a core part of the *qawwali* repertoire:

> The beauty sleeps on the bed, tresses covering the face,
> Let's go home, Khusraw, evening has set over the world.

Amir Khusraw himself died a few months later in Delhi and was buried near Nizamuddin Awliya's grave. His tomb as it stands now dates from Mughal times and has been added to and decorated at various times over the centuries. As stated earlier, the site is a place of pilgrimage and gatherings for devout pilgrims and sufis. The '*urs* or death anniversaries of Nizamuddin Awliya (18 Rabi' al-sani) and Amir Khusraw (17 Shawwal) are both occasions on which sufis from all over South Asia come together.

The tombs of the two luminaries are part and parcel of Delhi's landscape. In fact, in the novel *Twilight in Delhi* written in 1940 by Ahmed Ali, an elderly inhabitant of Delhi says while discussing the political downfall of the Mughals:

> The real causes of the loss of the Mughal Empire were some
> mistakes committed by the elders of that king, and the biggest
> of them all was that they had separated lover and beloved from
> each other by burying Hazrat Mahboob Elahi [Nizamuddin
> Awliya] and Hazrat Amir Khusro [in different graves]. The great
> love which existed between these two demanded that no
> curtain should be put between them. Because, Hazrat Mahboob
> Elahi used to say, that if the laws of Islam had not forbidden it he
> and Khusro would have been buried in the same grave.

Despite its political ups and downs, Amir Khusraw's beloved city Delhi has remained the capital of north Indian polities until modern times, and the few attempts to create alternative centers of power, such as Daulatabad in the Deccan by Muhammad Tughlaq in the fourteenth century and Agra and Fatehpur Sikri by the Lodhis and Mughals later, were unsuccessful in the long run.

3

AMIR KHUSRAW AND THE WORLD OF PERSIAN LITERATURE

PERSIAN LITERATURE IN INDIA

The first generation of Persian poets in India from the late eleventh and early twelfth centuries in Ghaznavid Lahore, such as Abu al-Faraj Runi and Mas'ud Sa'd Salman, continued the Persian literary traditions of the Samanid and early Ghaznavid courts in the poetic genres and imagery they employed. Of these two early poets, it is in the works of Mas'ud Sa'd Salman that we witness the earliest consciousness of a new poetics and the expansion of the traditional worldview to include the new cultures that they were occupying. These factors would give an impetus to the creation of a distinctly Indian Persian literature that lasted until the twentieth century. In the two centuries intervening between this time and that of Amir Khusraw, Persian poetry was written and cultivated in the subcontinent, most of it at the Ghaznavid court in Lahore, but much of this body of work is lost to us and only stray verses survive as quotations in historical chronicles or biographical dictionaries. The Mongol conquest caused many poets to seek refuge and find new sources of patronage at the courts of Uch and Delhi. It was here in around 1221 that the exiled poet 'Awfi wrote the earliest surviving biographical dictionary of Persian poets, *Lubab al-albab* (Quintessence of Hearts) that preserved the memory of the literary achievements of the past two centuries.

When Delhi became the capital city of the new rulers, it inherited many of the cultural institutions and literary practices of the Ghaznavids, causing a new literary florescence. The primary agents in this florescence were Amir Khusraw and Hasan. The former was extremely conscious of his multicultural heritage. From his mother he acquired knowledge of the local culture and language that translated into an abiding love for indigenous traditions. As a poet writing in Persian, he was aware of the larger world of Persian literary culture in which texts had a wide circulation across much of the non-Arab Islamic world. He writes with relish of the attractive quality of the Persian language, "Truly, the language of Fars is like pickles/For without pickles, food does not taste as good." Highly educated audiences in Shiraz, Isfahan, Balkh, and Bukhara read his poems, but he was also judged locally by Indian critics and by standards that may not have been universal, so he belonged to multiple worlds. It would appear that the Turk (the conqueror, lover) and the Hindu (the conquered slave, beloved), an extremely popular trope in Persian court poetry, came together in his person. As he says:

> The opposition has been removed from Turk and Hindu,
> For Hindustan has become one with Khurasan.

Greater Khurasan bridged the worlds of Iran and Central Asia and was the homeland of most of the Muslim settlers in India. Since Amir Khusraw was both of Turkish and Indian origins, he embodied the resolution of this conflict of opposites and a bridge between cultures, a phenomenon that would give a distinct identity to Indo-Persian literature.

Persian court poets of this time wrote their poems primarily in the form of the panegyric ode (*qasidah*), recited in praise of kings and princes on formal occasions at court. Many of Amir Khusraw's early *qasidah*s are in the style of the great Persian poets of the Ghaznavid and Seljuq periods, such as Farrukhi (d. 1037), Anvari (d. 1189), Khaqani (d. 1199), and Zahir (d. 1201), who served as models for fledgling court poets up to the nineteenth century. These odes are well-crafted poems written for ceremonial occasions and festivals such as the Iranian new year (*nawruz*) that were celebrated at Indian courts, and the Islamic 'Id al-Fitr and 'Id al-Azha. Poems in this genre allowed the poet to advertise his patron's virtues while at the same time discoursing about the relationship between himself and his patron, and between himself and the poets of the past. As he tells one patron in a *qasidah*:

> Even though I am the nightingale of words in the world's rose
>   garden,
> I flit about in this garden by the branch of your fortune.
> Don't forget me in the hunting place of your kindness,
> For crows and ravens eat the leftovers of royal falcons.

It was commonplace for poets to remind patrons about their loyalty and greatness, and on occasion even offer advice on proper kingly conduct. In a poem addressed to a nobleman, Amir Khusraw skillfully handles the imagery that is relevant to the courtly life of his time:

> Bravo illuminator of gatherings, if the north wind sees your
>   assembly,
> It will never carry the scent of roses, it will never take the
>   path to the garden!
>   If someone who is suffering passes through your assembly,
>   The boat of wine will carry him and he will find a shore
>   from the sea of sorrow.

> By the wind of your generosity, may the rain pour water in
>   the ocean,
> Out of envy of the cloud of your hand, the sun sets fire to the
>   mines.
>   The sun is your well-wisher and has its face in the sky,
>   Every dawn rises from it, taking its *qiblah* from it.
> As long as Hindustan exists in the world, and Khurasan as well,
> And if fortune is with someone, may he take both the former
>   and latter.
>   May Hindustan be in your possession and Khurasan too,
>   May victory which is with you take both of these.

All of nature is benevolent towards the nobleman who takes on its attributes such as generosity. The poem ends with a benediction that appears to be a tall order, since there was no question of attacking the area of Khurasan at all. Such exaggerated and profuse praise was a means to affirm the pact between patron and poet by setting high ideals in battle and banquet. Amir Khusraw also wrote many *qasidah*s in praise of Nizamuddin Awliya that are similarly solemn in tone but which draw on the mystical register of language.

POETICS OF THE SACRED AND PROFANE
GHAZAL

Amir Khusraw is better known today for his lyric poetry, in the form of *ghazal*s. This had become the most popular form during his lifetime because its language was easier than that of the *qasidah* and its primary subject was love. Love is treated in *ghazal*s in such an ambiguous way that the object of affection could be a beloved of any sex, since the Persian language does not indicate gender, and the setting for the feelings described could be earthly/courtly or mystical/sufi. In order to understand the subtle nature of this privileged genre of Persian poetry, one needs access to more than the poem itself, as explained by the scholar J.T.P. de Bruijn:

> The practice of love poetry in Persian in the tenth and eleventh centuries was initially purely secular. It seems that, during that period, ghazals were still mainly known as songs performed by minstrels...Since then, the fusion between the secular and the mystical in Persian ghazals has become such an essential characteristic that, in most instances, it is extremely difficult to make a proper distinction between the two. The decision whether a given poem should be called a Sufi ghazal or a profane love song very often does not depend so much on the poem itself, but on what we know about its writer, that is the answer to the question: does the life of the poet provide us with clues of a mystic affiliation, or is the poet only known as a court poet? (de Bruijn, 1997: 55)

In the case of a poet like Amir Khusraw, the challenge of contextualizing his poems is greater since he was active in both circles at once.

The first poem in Amir Khusraw's collection of poems (*divan*) is evocative of the Indian monsoon or a spring shower in a Persian garden:

> The clouds pour rain as I part from my beloved,
> What can I do on a day when I part from my beloved?
> The clouds and the rain, my beloved and I bid farewell,
> I weep alone, the cloud alone, my beloved alone.
> It is spring in the garden and a gentle breeze blows,
> The black-faced nightingale is bereft of the rose-garden.
> I do not want the blessing of sight from now on,
> Since the blessing of *that* vision is taken from me.
> > Your beauty will not endure since you left Khusraw,
> > A rose does not stay in bloom away from its thorns.

The poem is also reminiscent of a genre of Indian folksong where the beloved pines for her lover in the monsoon season, but here the poet has cleverly included the cloud as a participant in the drama of the lovers. In most *ghazals*, the poet/lover complains about separation from or the cruelty of his beloved. After lamenting sorrowfully in the poem, in the end the poet declares triumphantly that the beloved, and not he, will be harmed by this separation. There is a thematic unity and interconnectedness in this poem that is not characteristic of *ghazals* in subsequent centuries. The selection of lines in this poem, about half of the complete *ghazal*, reflects the choice made by singers who have rendered the piece vocally. What is more difficult to capture in translation is the way the rhyme word *juda* (separate) is used in multiple idiomatic expressions in every line of this poem.

As mentioned above, love is the central theme in the *ghazal* generally. In Amir Khusraw's poems it is a love informed by a courtly ethos that could equally be applied to mystical love for the divine. Often, the poems have homoerotic overtones and are addressed to a young boy, a literary convention in early Persian *ghazals* whose context was courtly banquets where pageboys and *saqis* were present, or sufi circles where there were beardless boys (*shahids*) whose beauty was a witness to the divine. Sometimes the poet speaks in the voice of an old man and chides himself for still being addicted to wine and boys, symbols for earthly snares that distract one from the mystical path.

Another feature of the *ghazal* that is regularly found in Amir Khusraw's poems is the sufi habit of taking an irreverent attitude towards the outer trappings of Islam that results in blasphemous utterances such as:

A person who is cautious and uses commonsense,
Don't listen to his words of love, for he is sober.

If your heart is not a target for the arrows of the beauties,
Step away from this circle, for the path is full of thorns.
O muezzin, you call me to the mosque,
Mind your own business, for mine is with wine and young lads.
A body on which the wind of desire does not blow is dead,
A heart in which there is no life is dead.
The old *ghazi* stains his beard red with blood while
I am an old sot and my dye is red wine.
I, a lost soul, am an idol-worshipper whom you call an ascetic,
The rosary that you see in my hand is a sacred thread.
> O Khursraw! A cold heart does not feel love's pains,
> It feels the sting of salt only in thoughts.

Only the poet/lover who thwarts the rules of society and religion and in the process becomes an infidel, i.e., Hindu in the Indian context and Christian or Zoroastrian in the Iranian, is able to traverse the true path of love. By drinking wine and dallying with young lads, he breaks the norms of tradition, as represented by narrow-minded practitioners of religion like the muezzin and *ghazi*.

Although the ideas and sentiments expressed here come close to those found in the extensive corpus of such a poet as Rumi, these poems are not spontaneous outbursts but carefully crafted pieces, with a simple elegance that can be appreciated by all kinds of urban audiences. Amir Khusraw knows that the language of love is universal, yet understood by a select few:

> Speaking about the mysteries of love to the cold-hearted
> Is like speaking Hindavi in Kashghar and Khotan!

The fact that many of his poems have sufi overtones does not necessarily mean that all his lyrics should be viewed as mystical. Sufi terminology and imagery had permeated lyric poetry to such an extent that distinctions between secular and mystical poetry were no longer valid. As a craftsman, Amir Khusraw was well aware of his predecessors and consciously imitated them. His main predecessors in the genre of *ghazal* were Sa'di, who did not write mystical poems, and 'Iraqi, whose verses are entirely sufi, and his own poems draw from both types. The fact that some of his poems are part of the practice of Sufism today does render them mystical in the context of performance but may not have been so originally. Medieval Persian poetry functioned at several levels, and in this poem the levels are both mystical and secular:

> Your pure body under a shirt,
> By God! what a body it is.
> Your shirt is like a drop of water
> That sits tightly on the rose and jasmine.
> Pull me to yourself inside the garment,
> For you are life and my life your body.
> As long as I live, I will tear off my clothes in my love for you,
> For after death, it is the turn of the shroud.
> You have stolen many hearts, know this well,
> Mine is more wounded than the others.
> Come in and live in my soul,
> For you are life and your life is your body.
> You said, I will not leave you,
> My Turk, what is the need for these words?
> Your mouth shut tight, your face open,
> How do you keep talking, after all, what is this art?
> > Khusraw's heart is content with narrowness,
> > Since he remembers that mouth of yours.

The erotic element in this poem can be taken both literally and as a metaphor for longing for union with the divine. The beloved remains characteristically aloof and unresponsive and the poet is content to survive on the hope of an eventual union.

The following *ghazal* of Amir Khusraw in praise of the Prophet Muhammad, which is extremely popular in *qawwali* performances, can only be interpreted in a mystical sense. According to Bruce Lawrence, whose translation appears below, "He recounts an indescribable moment with the dramatic refrain 'in that place where I was last night,' alluding to the spiritual transport often experienced by participants in the mystical 'audition' called *sama'*."

> I do not know what abode it was, that place where I was last
>   night.
> On every side I saw the dance of the *bismil* ("in the name of
>   God"), in that place where I was last night.
> I saw one with the form of an angel, the height of a cypress,
>   cheeks like tulips,
> From head to toe I quivered, my heart astir, in that place
>   where I was last night.
> Rivals, listen to that voice, the voice which calms my raging
>   fright.
> The words he spoke left me in awe, in that place where I was
>   last night.
> Muhammad was the candle illuminating the assembly,
>   O Khusraw, in that place which was no place.
> And God himself was the head of that gathering, in that place
>   where I was last night. (Renard, 1998: 347, 349)

This poem and many others are still sung by Afghan and Indian artistes, either in a mystical or secular setting. Precisely what criteria played a role in a poem being performed in a mystical setting is not an easy question to answer. Any *ghazal* of Amir Khusraw can be considered mystical depending on the context in which it is sung, and the poet may consciously have written some *ghazals* exclusively for use in sufi gatherings at Nizamuddin Awliya's *jama'atkhanah*; others were meant for a more courtly audience, but some were bound to be used in both contexts based on their appeal for contemporary audiences.

Nizamuddin Awliya is reported to have said about the effects of *ghazal*s and other forms of verse:

> Each individual must grasp the connotation of poems for himself. Consider the case of Shaykh al-Islam Farid ad-din – may God sanctify his lofty secret. Once the following verses came on his blessed lips:
>
> > O Nizami, what secrets are these, revealed from your heart?
> > His secret no one knows; bridle your tongue! Bridle your tongue!
>
> Throughout most of the day, right up till the time of evening prayer, he kept reciting this couplet. At the breaking of fast the same couplet remained on his blessed lips. It is reported that at dawn the following day he was still repeating this couplet, and each time he uttered it his countenance changed. (Hasan Sijzi, 1992: 198)

The involvement of sufis in popularizing the *ghazal* form among the masses is corroborated by another disciple of Nizamuddin Awliya, Amir Khurd, who writes, "All the *qawwal*s of the city looked to the refined nature of that monarch of love and inventor of the art of music, and kept employing his new *ghazal*s and new tunes and raised the art of song to that of the higher sciences."

The popularity of Urdu *ghazal*s today among South Asians around the world provides an example of the viability and universal appeal of this poetic form. This ultimately has roots in the Indo-Persian *ghazal* of a few centuries after Amir Khusraw, although he is often considered to have established the tradition. There is a vast corpus of Persian *ghazal*s authored by Amir Khusraw, 1,726 in the last edition of his poems published in Tehran, and the few that are performed today probably have long been popular in an oral setting. It is also to be expected that in an environment where orality was the privileged form of disseminating a text, there would be some degree of mis-attribution or confusion, as in the case of this couplet:

> Every community has its own path of religion and place of
> prayer,
> I have set my *qiblah* in the direction of the one with his cap
> awry.

The young boy with his cap awry is actually the divine beloved in a mystical interpretation of the poem. The context of this verse is thought to be an exchange between Nizamuddin Awliya, to whom the first line is attributed, and Amir Khusraw, who replied with the second line. However, the entire *ghazal* is found in Hasan's *divan*, but the misattribution to Khusraw persists because the world of these three individuals was so inextricably linked, and was made more so in the history of the reception of the texts associated with them. In the seventeenth century, the Mughal emperor Jahangir (r. 1605–16) narrates in his memoirs, *Tuzuk-i Jahangiri*, that during a *qawwali* session at court when this line was being performed, the singer expired while trying to explain the subtleties of its meaning! Another well-known verse from a *ghazal* by Amir Khusraw is the following, which is believed to represent the deep bond between poet and *pir* that made them one entity:

> I have become you, you have become me.
> I have become life, you have become body.
> From now on, let no one say that
> I am other and you are another.

This is not an unusual couplet in the context of the entire poem, but it has taken on a life of its own and developed into an emblematic sufi text.

Defining Amir Khusraw's corpus is a philological problem complicated by the vastness of his *oeuvre* and his use of more than one language. In the introduction to his third *divan*, he writes, "None of the sovereigns of poetry before had three *divan*s, only I, who am the king [Khusraw] of the kingdom of discourse. Although Mas'ud Sa'd Salman did have three *divan*s, they are in Arabic, Persian and Hindavi." Although here he only mentions his Persian verse, elsewhere he refers to his poetry in Arabic and Hindavi. His Arabic poems are few and scattered in his prose writings, while the question of his Hindavi poetry will be taken up in the next section.

Amir Khusraw compiled at least four collections of his Persian lyric and panegyric poetry, excluding the long narrative poems, from different periods of his life, with a fifth compiled posthumously: *Tuhfat al-sighar* (Gift of Youth) compiled in 1273; *Vasat al-hayat* (Middle of Life) in 1284; *Ghurrat al-kamal* (Prime of Perfection) in 1294; *Baqiyah naqiyah* (Miscellaneous Selections) in 1316; and *Nihayat al-jamal* (Extremity of Beauty) in 1325, perhaps after his death. None of these are available in their complete form in modern critical editions. The collections of his poetry published in India and Iran are actually selections from all the five *divan*s. Amir Khusraw also wrote introductions to his five *divan*s of poetry; these have not been published with the modern editions of his poems. The introduction to the third collection, which is known as the *Dibachah-i divan-i ghurrat-i kamal*, is both a treatise on poetry and autobiography of his poetic self. It remains the primary source of information about his life.

As the corpus of Persian poetry received became too large to be copied and read, people found creative ways to incorporate texts that continued to appeal to them. One example is a seventeenth-century oil torch with Amir Khusraw's lyrics engraved on it, which not only provides proof of the poet's popularity at a later date but also of the way that courtly literature formed part of the material culture of the period. His *ghazals* continued to be sung, but the manuscripts of these collections were not usually furnished with illustrations. Instead, selected lines were calligraphed and collected in albums filled with specimens of the work of master painters and calligraphers. Each line of a *ghazal* is considered to be an independent unit, and therefore couplets from a poem were chosen to be recited and/or calligraphed on the basis of their appeal to an audience. Such practices allowed for the memory of poets and artists to be kept alive at different times in history.

Amir Khusraw's *ghazals* have had a great impact on later poets, including the master poet of this genre, Hafiz of Shiraz

Amir Khusraw's poem in a calligraphic panel.

(d. 1391). They have a continuous oral tradition to this day, especially in Central and South Asia, even though Persian is no longer widely understood in the latter region. But in Amir Khusraw's time, it was actually his friend Hasan who was considered the master of the *ghazal* and was given the title "Sa'di of India." According to their contemporary Nasiruddin Chiragh-i Dehli, however, neither poet succeeded in matching Sa'di's standards. A Persian poet and literary historian from Harat, Jami (d. 1492), quotes Hasan on the subject of professional rivalry between the poets:

> May Khusraw accept graciously
> What *I*, Hasan, compose,
> My poetry is not like that by Khusraw,
> Poetry is this which *I* compose.

Literary judgments change over time since they are dictated by prevailing aesthetic and artistic trends. Amir Khusraw himself says in homage to the *ghazal*s of Sa'di of Shiraz in the following verse:

> Khusraw poured into the goblet of meaning,
> A drink from the tavern of intoxication in Shiraz.

He was so conscious of producing works in every genre used by the Iranian masters that it is somewhat surprising that he did not attempt to imitate Sa'di's didactic works, the *Gulistan* (Rose Garden) and *Bustan* (Scented Garden), which are masterpieces of Persian literature and have been imitated by numerous authors over time.

Modern literary critics of Persian poetry often claim that the so-called "Indian style" (*sabk-i Hindi*) of Persian lyric poetry, which is characterized by elaborate metaphors and an abstractness, has its origins in the verses of Amir Khusraw. This style of poetry was in vogue in the entire Persianate world a couple of centuries after Amir Khusraw, especially among Mughal poets in India, including classical Urdu poets, and Amir Khusraw was indeed widely read and imitated by poets who propounded this style. Therefore, a claim that seeks to ascribe the origins of a later literary movement to an earlier poet can be interpreted as connecting the "Indian"-ness of this body of poetry to an earlier Indo-Persian poet par excellence, and has less to do with stylistics and more with forging symbolic origins to a nascent literary culture. Amir Khusraw's *ghazals* are more like those of the poets of his own time, mainly Sa'di and Hasan, and inspired later poets who worked with the trends and ideals of their own time. It would be incorrect to claim that he started a new style of lyric poetry.

The two qualities in poetry that were prized by Amir Khusraw were *ravani* (fluency) and *iham* (*double entendre* or punning). *Ravani* was prized by many medieval Persian poets who aimed at an easy, yet elegant, style. Amir Khusraw explicitly says that the style of a great poet should be simple (not like that of preachers), free of errors, and original. His classification of the *ghazals* he has written reflects the gradual development of a poetic temperament: he likens the *ghazals* of his first *divan* to the earth because they are cold and dry in their formality; those of his second *divan* are like water, gentle, soft, and purged of the dust of all dense words; those in the third category are *ghazals* that are roasted and baked to perfection but delicate at the same time, and are to be found in his *divan* that is appropriately called "Prime of Perfection"; his fourth *divan* has *ghazals* that like fire can set alight a heart that is cold and devoid of passion. The second desirable quality in poetry, *iham*, is a particular favorite of Amir Khusraw and is one of the identifying characteristics of his unique style, as will be discussed later.

LEGEND AND HISTORY IN NARRATIVE POETRY

By Amir Khusraw's time, there had been several major poets who would form the core of the canon of classical Persian literature. Sa'di has been mentioned above as a master poet of love lyrics and didactic literature who was greatly admired by all Persian poets, but perhaps no one had taken the literary world of Persia by storm as the two poets Firdawsi (d. 1020) with his Iranian epic, *Shahnamah* (Book of Kings) and Nizami (d. 1209) with his quintet of narrative poems, the *khamsah*. Both poets composed heroic or romantic tales in the *masnavi* form, but implicitly dealt with issues of morality, kingship, and courtly love. They had a universal appeal in the eastern Islamic world, and the *Shahnamah*, dealing with pre-Islamic kings of Iran, was especially popular in the Persianate courts because it espoused Iranian ideals of kingship and ethical behavior. The commissioning of a new copy of this text with illustrations came to be regarded as a symbolic act that conferred legitimacy on a new ruler. Therefore, innumerable manuscripts of this text have survived from courts in every corner of the Persianate world. Poets also tried to imitate the *Shahnamah*, with the express purpose of rivaling Firdawsi. The story of the Ghaznavid sultan Mahmud's role in commissioning this work from the great poet was well known, and poets saw themselves as recreating Firdawsi's role every time they wrote a similar poem.

Nizami's influence on poets who wrote *masnavi*s was just as extensive, and poets imitated his work innumerable times. If Firdawsi's *Shahnamah* was a source of political legitimacy, Nizami's *khamsah* was one of cultural prestige. The five works in the *khamsah* contained all the elements that were part and parcel of the Persian literary universe: Iranian and

Arab romantic legends, the pre-Islamic Iranian historical past, and didactic and philosophical discourses, all which came to be accepted as the epitome of the civilization's cultural achievement. Amir Khusraw was the first poet who set out to match Nizami's achievements, not to outdo him but rather to measure up to his standard by producing works that would be more relevant to his own milieu. No one has surpassed Nizami in the beauty of his language and the subtlety of his thoughts. Amir Khusraw's strengths lay in his fast-paced narrative and lightheartedness, and his fondness for wordplay and *double entendre*. In these poems, he was able to express himself fully as a story-teller. He himself compares his accomplishments to those of the great master at the conclusion of the work:

If honey is useful,
Vinegar too has its buyers.
If a pearl is expensive,
Amber too has value.
This work is without blemish,
Although not golden, it has glitter.

Elsewhere, with regard to the material he has to work with and knowing that he will be compared to his great predecessor, Amir Khusraw playfully complains that Nizami had consumed the fine wine from the goblet of the subject matter of the stories, and left the dregs for the other poets.

Whereas Nizami had painstakingly crafted each poem at a slow pace, Amir Khusraw's *khamsah* was written quickly, between the years 1298 and 1302. Each poem bears dedications to both Sultan 'Alauddin Khalji and Nizamuddin Awliya, each of them his patron in their own way. A younger contemporary of Amir Khusraw, 'Isami (d. 1350), wrote a history of

Islam in India in epic format, in which he explains the genesis of
his work and pays tribute to his models:

> Two poets, expert in the art of *masnavi*,
> Have achieved perfection in the world.
> One, Firdawsi, made a peacock manifest itself
> And adorned Tus like paradise.
> The second, Nizami, made a nightingale sing
> And graced the garden of Ganjah.
> I followed both of them
> And became the disciple of both in the *masnavi*.
> From the peacock and nightingale, in India,
> A melodious parrot, Khusraw, was born.

In this way, Amir Khusraw became a prominent figure in
Persian literary history, and many later poets who wrote *mas-
navis* had similar stories of how they were inspired by their predecessors, sometimes even preferring the poet of Delhi to the
one from Ganjah.

As part of his quintet, Amir Khusraw wrote his versions of
the two most popular romances, *Shirin and Khusraw*, a story set
in pre-Islamic Iran, and *Majnun and Layla*, a legend from Arabia.
He inverted the order of the names of the lovers in the titles to
distinguish his versions from those of Nizami, but did not
change the basic plots of the stories, although there are a few
new elements in the order of the events and portrayal of characters. The first story is set in the pre-Islamic Iranian past but
is more of a legend than historical truth. Khusraw Parviz
(r. 590–628), the namesake of our poet, was the Sassanian ruler
of Iran, while Shirin was an Armenian princess. The two fall in
love early on but are separated for a long time by Khusraw's
involvement in military campaigns and his short-lived
marriages to Maryam, the Byzantine princess, and Shikar, a
slave girl. In the meantime, Shirin is the object of an ardent love

by Farhad, a sculptor and the son of the emperor of China in this version. Both Khusraw and Shirin have their respective rivals murdered, and they marry, but their union is not longlasting because Khusraw is killed by his son Shiruyah, who wants to marry Shirin, who commits suicide over Khusraw's grave on her wedding day. The whole work is a metaphorical commentary on proper kingship, a highly charged issue at that time.

Majnun and Layla, the story of Qays and Layla, is set among the nomadic tribes of the deserts of Arabia. The two fall in love when they are children at school, but their relationship is not approved of by society. Qays spends much of his time in the wilderness and becomes a madman (Majnun); he has animals as his companions and is wasting away in his love. Layla (or Layli in Persian) is also pining for her lover; when she hears a false rumor about his death, she falls ill and dies. When she is being buried, Majnun jumps into the grave and dies clutching the body of his beloved. Majnun's behavior is extreme in every

Majnun at Layla's grave.

respect and his character possesses all the qualities of a typical
lover in *ghazal* poetry. The intensity of his passion transcends
cultural boundaries and has immortalized this story not just in
the Middle East, but also in South Asia and beyond. Especially
in sufi poetry, the character of Majnun is given a mystical spin,
symbolizing martyrdom in the path of love.

The lovers in the stories just discussed remain the epitomes
of romantic love in Persianate literature to this day. On a
broader level, the romances of Nizami and Amir Khusraw
explore, in the words of Julie S. Meisami, "the relationship
between love and justice, and specifically the role of love as the
source of that wisdom which leads both to justice and to universal harmony." (Meisami, 1987: 182–3.) Subsequent poets in the
Persianate traditions not only imitated the two poets in retelling
the stories but also translated or used them as models for local
love stories in other related literary cultures, such as Ottoman
and Chaghatay Turkish, and Urdu. Amir Khusraw's versions vary
in plot and stylistics from those of Nizami. There is less emphasis on the development of characters and more on moving the
plot forward. For instance, in the story of Khusraw and Shirin,
Amir Khusraw gives a bigger role to Farhad, portraying him
exactly like Majnun, a passionate and devoted lover, and his
character overshadows the others. Nizami is also more sympa-
thetic towards his women protagonists and critical of the male
characters. Both poets provide personal information in their
poems, usually at the beginning or end, in the form of offering
advice to their children or mourning the loss of loved ones.

The popular narrative of Alexander's exploits has its origins
in Hellenistic texts that passed into Persian and existed in prose
as well as in verse. Both Nizami and Amir Khusraw versified this
story; the former's work is entitled *Iskandarnamah* (Book of
Alexander), while the latter's version is called the *A'inah-i
Iskandari* (The Alexandrine Mirror). The plot of the *A'inah-i*

Iskandari is convoluted and involves the adventures of Alexander the Great, considered to be a prophet in Islam, while he was on his campaigns in the east. In his version of the story, Amir Khusraw sought to take Alexander further than Nizami had done. Even Nizami's version is considered problematic since it is neither a romance about two lovers nor a genuine epic, but rather combines elements of both. In Nizami's portrayal of the legendary hero the emphasis is on justice and kingship with long passages of psychological analysis and philosophical discourse involving Plato and Aristotle, along with epic-style encounters with the Russians, Chinese, and an Amazon warrior. Alexander's true adventure is narrated in the second half of the poem where he searches for the water of life and encounters the prophet Khizr. Amir Khusraw declares at the beginning of his work that his story will be different. His Alexander is not so much a prophet and philosopher as an adventurer or even a scientist. In the technical details concerning the astrolabe and the art of glassmaking found in this work, Amir Khusraw reveals an expert's knowledge that goes beyond a superficial manipulation of imagery. His Alexander's quest for the water of life is as much a spiritual journey as an attempt to measure the depth of the ocean.

The other two of Nizami's works in his quintet, the first and the last in the set, are the *Makhzan al-asrar* (Treasury of Secrets), consisting of short parables illustrating ethical and spiritual concerns, and the *Haft paykar* (Seven Beauties), which is a collection of stories told to the Iranian king Bahram Gur by seven princesses associated with seven different colors, who represent the different climes of the world. It was in these two works, which required the inclusion of new stories and action-filled narratives, that Amir Khusraw was able to exercise his own literary expertise in choosing the material. Of the twenty tales in Amir Khusraw's *Matla' al-anvar* (Rising of

Lights), some are from Islamic lore, while others are more general. One story that fits the cultural context of the poet, and is often illustrated in manuscripts of this work, is of a pious Brahman who is crawling towards his idol and impresses a Muslim pilgrim with his devotion, and by example educates him about Islam.

In his *Hasht bihisht* (Eight Paradises), which has one more tale than Nizami's work, the stories that the eight princesses tell Bahram Gur are longer, faster paced than in Nizami's, full of witty wordplay and with complex plots that involve magic and adventure. The details in the tales show that the poet is certainly drawing on his Indian background by including stories that he would have heard orally. One of these stories, the one that the Tatar princess Gulnari narrates to Bahram Gur on Tuesday in the red pavilion, appears in an English translation in Appendix II. The translation attempts to convey some of the flavor of Amir Khusraw's original text; the narrative technique and literary devices are typical of his style in general. As always, the background of his story is India, with many stock images associated with the land.

Amir Khusraw's *khamsah* was read and imitated by later poets as assiduously as Nizami's and, due to the rich content of its stories, was often illustrated. Each illustrated manuscript of this work reflects local artistic trends and the tastes of patrons, and the interest the work elicited at a particular historical moment. Looking at the distribution of manuscript production of the works of an author also helps in mapping the extent of dissemination and influence of his writings. The earliest copies of the *khamsah* are from central India, dating from the early to mid-fifteenth century, with illustrations that are simple and in a local style, and bearing great similarity to Jain manuscript paintings from western India. A deluxe edition of Amir Khusraw's *khamsah* with illustrations in the high Mughal style was produced at the emperor Akbar's court (r. 1556–1605). In the sixteenth and seventeenth centuries, the Mughals had a large-scale program of preserving the cultural legacy of India through the copying and refinishing of many Persian texts, in addition to commissioning translations of works from Sanskrit. It was not just the Mughals who were interested in this *khamsah*. There are numerous copies of this quintet from Iran, Central Asia, and Turkey. At the Institute of Oriental Studies in Uzbekistan, there is even a copy of Amir Khusraw's *khamsah* dating from 1355 in the handwriting of the most revered Iranian poet, Hafiz of Shiraz, this being the highest compliment one poet could pay another, apart from imitating his style.

Amir Khusraw wrote his *khamsah* as a tribute to Nizami and in order to establish his standing as a poet. Once he had completed it, he returned to something he had tried earlier: writing narrative poetry using actual events of his time as the plot. His purpose here was to achieve something that would distinguish him in Persian literary history as an innovator rather than an imitator. At this time, Persian poets were moving towards the adoption of the narrative *masnavi* form instead of the panegyric ode (*qasidah*). Narrative poetry in Persian usually dealt with epic and romantic legends from past history, taken up to address issues of concern specifically from the author's own time. Amir Khusraw's personal engagement with the court and the political events of his time, by contrast, allowed him to present living history through the lens of fiction and didactic poetry. He wrote five *masnavi*s, one in the reign of each sultan that he served, all dealing with the courtly side of his life. None of them included any events of his own personal life or the world around Nizamuddin Awliya, although by dedicating each one to the latter he was bridging the gap between the royal court and the sufi *khanaqah*. Modern critics have a hard time with works of this historical narrative genre because they are neither purely historical nor purely poetic texts. The truth is that each work stands on its own, and they are of uneven quality. Although the genre of historical poems may be problematic for historians who use them as sources for the history of the period, as literary artifacts the works are a fascinating subject of study.

The subject of his narrative poem the *Qiran al-sa'dayn* is the falling out and reconciliation between Bughra Khan and his son, the sultan Kayqubad. A shorter and less ambitious work, *Miftah al-futuh*, completed two years later, describes four successful military campaigns undertaken by Sultan Jalaluddin Khalji in one year. In both of these poems written to glorify the exploits of his patrons, Amir Khusraw emphasizes the fact that he is reporting the truth without any hyperbole, but these are not an objective historical documentation of the events that transpired. Rather they are hybrid forms of poetry, containing panegyric elements combined with characteristics of epic. Interspersed in the narrative are vignettes about courtly life and descriptions of architectural monuments and cities that add to the historical quality of the works. The following is a description from *Miftah al-futuh* of the palace of the rajah of Jhayin and the temples there at the time of Jalaluddin Khalji's conquest in 1291:

> He alighted at the Rajah's private palace,
> Which was a skyscraper in its loftiness.
> What did he see but a garden grown out of stone!
> The pictures in Azhang[1] fell short of it.
> A painted palace of hard stone,
> A manifestation of the paradise of the Hindus.

1. An ideal beautiful object, a picture book painted by the mythical master artist Mani.

In portraiture like a Chinese painting,
The imagination was lost in seeing it.
It was not a form painted by a human brush!
It wiped out the pictures of Mani.
A hundred Byzantine figures in ornate stone,
Made in a way that no one could do with wax.
The plaster on the walls were virtual mirrors,
In which the reflection of people was like a mural.

The imagery and rhetorical devices employed here are the same as in his fictional tales, such as that in Appendix II, and the boundaries between "historical" and "romantic" narratives begin to blend. In these so-called historical accounts, the vaunting of the poet with respect to the massacre of infidels (*kafir*s) and destruction of idol-temples must be understood in the context of the genre of the work. It was commonplace for poets to indulge in hyperbole and present events using the cliched language of epic. These poems are not supposed to be read as reports of actual occurrences. Amir Khusraw is successful in his innovation of a new poetic genre, one that had not been attempted quite in this way before, but which troubles us as modern readers since it does not fall neatly into any of the familiar categories of poetic texts.

The third historical poem, *'Ashiqah* (Beloved), also known by the title *'Ishqiyah* (Love Story), which Amir Khusraw says is modeled after Layla and Majnun, is the symbolic union of the two major Indian traditions that produced a rich culture whose history begins with the poet himself. The *'Ishqiyah* was completed in 1315, more than a decade after he had written his *khamsah*. It is probably his best-known work among the historical narrative poems and the one most often illustrated. The theme of this poem is as fabulous as any legend or mythical tale, describing the love of Sultan 'Alauddin's son, the young prince Khizr Khan, for the Hindu princess Devaldi, who was the daughter of Raja

Karan of Gujarat. Khizr Khan was a well-liked and admired prince who was also a disciple of Nizamuddin Awliya. For these reasons, Amir Khusraw must have been personally close to him. After the conquest of Gujarat in 1297 by Ulugh Khan, Princess Devaldi was brought to Delhi and raised in the royal harem. In a fairytale turn of events, the two fell in love, and despite the designs of the prince's mother to keep them apart, they were united in marriage. This is the point where Amir Khusraw had ended his romance, but in fact the lovers had a tragic end when Khizr Khan was imprisoned, blinded, and finally killed in the fort of Gwalior by his brother Mubarak Shah in his bid for the throne. After the four years of this sultan's rule were over, Amir Khusraw updated the narrative and ended the tale on a sad note.

Amir Khusraw declares that he wanted to create an Indian love story to match the legendary tales of star-crossed lovers such as Vis and Ramin, Vamiq and Azra, and Layla and Majnun. Engaging in his usual wordplay, he says that the name of the princess was Deval, which he changed to Duval Rani because *duval* is the plural of *dawlat* (fortune) and she was the queen of great fortune. In laying out the background for the story, the poet gives a short history of Muslim rulers and Islamic civilization in India, which culminates in the union of the two lovers who symbolically represent the synthesis of the two major cultures of the land. The work is in the form of the two lovers addressing each other in a continuous dialogue, interspersed with didactic anecdotes. The spirit of this work accorded with that of the early Mughals, and therefore a copy of this work was produced in the royal atelier during Akbar's reign.

The *Nuh sipihr* (Nine Heavens), also called *Sultannamah* (Book of the Sultan), is a literary *tour de force* that has never been matched in the history of Persian literature. Written for the young sultan Mubarak Shah, it is a collection of unconnected vignettes about different aspects of courtly life, like the poet's first historical *masnavi*. The vignettes are on topics such as the sultan's accession to the throne, the birth of his son, the architectural projects he patronized, and a hunting trip, and the work includes discourses about subjects such as kingship, the art of poetry, and Indian culture. It is known today largely for the factual information it contains, but it is equally of interest for its unusual form. Instead of a frame story or a single narrative, the poet has used a more systematic organizing device by dividing the work into nine sections, each corresponding to the seven planets and the sun and moon, each one in a different poetic meter and concluding with an address to a *saqi* and a *ghazal*. The often-cited detailed description of India in section three is an ingenious eulogy to the land of his birth and is discussed below.

Amir Khusraw's last poem on a historical subject, the *Tughlaqnamah*, was mentioned above as describing a low point in the history of Delhi that can only be compared to ancient Rome at its most debauched and violent period. This work describes the heroic efforts of Ghiyasuddin Tughlaq to rescue the throne of Delhi from the usurper Khusraw Khan, who deposed Sultan Mubarak Shah and became the ruler for a few months. Many scholars have criticized this work and other poems of this genre as being insincere and mercenary, saying that if Khusraw Khan had defeated Ghiyasuddin Tughlaq and remained sultan, Amir Khusraw would have celebrated *him* in an epic poem. It must be kept in mind that the court poet was hired precisely to praise his patron. When he did not see praiseworthy qualities in the patron, a powerful and capable poet would gently offer advice on the correct behavior of a Muslim king or prince and present an idealized picture of the situation in order to provide an exemplary model. Poetry or praise was not meant to reflect the direct or sincere feelings of the poet; it is in the moralizing sections in the narrative where reality is to be found.

The historical poems comprise a vast body of poetry for any individual to have produced, yet it only represents part of Amir Khusraw's entire corpus. The modern reader almost automatically questions the quality of a poet who wrote so profusely, but this is a judgment that must be made on an individual basis. The fact remains that even in pre-modern times, the literati were grappling with the large corpus of the poet's works. The fifteenth-century literary biographer of Persian poets, Dawlatshah, writing in Herat, is effusive about Amir Khusraw's poetry and states that his patron, the Timurid prince Sultan Baysunghur Mirza, who supposedly preferred Khusraw's *khamsah* to that of Nizami, made an attempt to have all of Amir Khusraw's poetry collected but gave up the idea when faced with the daunting body of his work. Thus, even a couple of centuries after his death, only a selection of the complete works of the poet was available in particular collections.

As was mentioned above, Amir Khusraw's works were extremely popular at the Mughal court. These works did not merely have symbolic value for the Mughals who attempted to preserve what they could of the Indo-Persian heritage and give a distinct identity to them, but they were also a source of information about the past. When the Mughal historian 'Abd al-Qadir Bada'uni wrote the *Muntakhab al-tavarikh* (Selection of Histories), much of his data about the thirteenth- and early fourteenth-century Sultanate history came from Amir Khusraw's historical narratives. Amir Khusraw is the only source we have for many of the events of his times. The history of the contemporary chronicler Kabiruddin is lost to us, while Barni, the author of the useful *Tarikh-i Firuzshahi* (History of Firuzshah), describes these events a generation later. In an exciting bibliographical turn of events, during the time of the Mughal emperor Akbar, it was discovered that the imperial copy of the *Tughlaqnamah* was missing some pages from the beginning and end. After an unsuccessful attempt to locate a complete copy during the reign of the next ruler, Jahangir, the Iranian émigré poet Hayati Gilani was commissioned to complete the missing sections. The poet did so and dedicated the "new" work to both Nizami and Amir Khusraw.

If it is surprising that Amir Khusraw did not attempt to write a national epic of India, an equivalent of the *Shahnamah*, one of his younger contemporaries would do the job. 'Isami wrote the *Futuh al-salatin* (Victories of the Sultans), a history of Muslim rule in India in verse, subtitled the *Shahnamah* of India!

PROSE WORKS

In keeping with his literary versatility and creativity, Amir Khusraw also wrote some prose works that have not been as popular as his poetry or had much of an impact on Indo-Persian writers after him. Not every poet was a writer of prose, and the forms of prose and poetry were accorded different degrees of respect. Hasan reports on Nizamuddin Awliya's views on the two forms, "Every eloquent turn of phrase that one hears causes delight but the same thought expressed in prose when cast into verse causes still greater delight" (Hasan Sijzi, 1992: 154). There was a definite preference for verse in pre-modern Persianate cultures, and no prose work was devoid of poetic quotations.

Several works in prose are attributed to Amir Khusraw but it can be said on the basis of scholarly analysis that they date from a later time. The chief of these are the sufi text *Afzal al-fava'id* (Most Excellent Morals), the Persian–Hindi dictionary *Khaliq bari*, and the *Tale of the Four Dervishes*. In addition to the prose introductions to his *divans*, Amir Khusraw wrote two works in prose. The *Khaza'in al-futuh* is a chronicle describing the military exploits of 'Alauddin Khalji, written in a florid and

highly rhetorical style. This work does not conform to the
pattern of traditional historical chronicles and is a rhetorical
exercise in writing prose. It has even been suggested in recent
years that prose was not the author's forte and that this is the
reason for the paucity of his writings in this form. Amir Khusraw
was first and foremost a poet and even in writing historical verse
narratives, he did not claim to be a historian. He was a literary
genius who mixed forms and genres and even the one prose
chronicle he composed is extremely poetic. In fact, the tradition
of Indo-Persian prose writing from before Amir Khusraw, as in
Hasan Nizami's *Taj al-ma'asir*, is a new form of writing that
employs the metaphorical language of poetry in prose form to
an extreme level.

His major prose work, *I'jaz-i Khusravi* (Miracle of Khusraw),
also known as *Rasa'il al-i'jaz* (The Miraculous Treatises), is a
massive compilation in five books of model prose writings in
the forms of letters and anecdotes. The entire work is written
in such a complex style that only a specialist can comprehend
them, let alone appreciate the intricate rhetorical devices and
wordplay employed by the author. Unfortunately, this work,
like his poetry, has not been published in a critical edition, and
the nineteenth-century lithographed version from India is a
rare item in libraries around the world. Amir Khusraw's writings in this miscellany impressively range from a *farman* (royal
decree) drafted by him for Sultan 'Alauddin Khalji addressed to
Farid Khan, the governor of Ma'bar some time in 1310–11, to
jokes of a bawdy nature. The following piece, a satire on a sufi
gathering, which may not seem an appropriate subject from
Amir Khusraw's pen, reveals the place of humor in pre-modern
attitudes towards subjects that are often sanctified in our times:

> The *sama'* assembly had grown warm when the fellow Latif
> let loose, waving his arms around, and the so-called Shah

who was lame, kept stomping the ground until he was so overcome by emotion that he wanted to take his trousers off and throw them at the minstrel. On one side the trousers came off easily, but on the other side where the opening was narrow, they wouldn't come off. In this way, he kept pulling at them and dancing on his lame foot. His enthusiasm affected the others greatly.

As we become better acquainted with Amir Khusraw's writings, it can be seen that he was accomplished in many fields other than poetry, such as science and music, all of which he employed in some way in his writings. He describes the relationship between general knowledge and poetry thus, "Knowledge remains veiled by the minutiae of facts, while poetry becomes well-known due to the manipulation of facts." As for the art of versification, he says,

> Poetry is higher than wisdom and wisdom lies at the bottom of poetry. A poet can be called a wise man but a wise man cannot be called a poet. Magic is considered part of rhetoric but rhetoric is not magic. Therefore, a poet can be called a magician but a magician cannot be called a poet.

A detailed study of Amir Khusraw's theory of poetry and aesthetics would do much to advance the state of scholarship on his works. However, his views on the subject of poetry are not found only in the realm of theory. To get a more complete picture of him as a poet, it is necessary to understand his relationship to the local world around him and be grounded in traditions that endure to our day.

4

AMIR KHUSRAW AND INDIAN CULTURAL TRADITIONS

MUSIC AND *QAWWALI*

In modern South Asia, Amir Khusraw is chiefly remembered for his involvement in music and vernacular compositions in the Hindavi language. It is fair to declare at the outset that Amir Khusraw's musical compositions and vernacular writings are mostly his by attribution and that the written traditions of these texts date from several centuries after he lived. However, they survive as his cultural legacy and the spirit embedded in these works is unmistakably that of the poet, and thus they must be treated as serious subjects of study. Amir Khusraw's Persian works are now more widely accessible in the world beyond South Asia, but for the most part, except through secondary sources and translations, no longer so in the region itself due to the loss of Persian as a language of learning. Therefore, the portion of his creative output that only pertains to South Asia, i.e., his vernacular compositions, becomes doubly valuable in that context.

Early biographers of Amir Khusraw corroborate his deep interest in and involvement with the world of music. Although details about his exact contribution to this field, in the way of theoretical writings on musicology or innovations with instruments, are lacking in the sources of his time and may never be known to us, there is ample evidence in Amir Khusraw's own writings that he had more than a cursory interest in music. In this short poem from his *divan*, he compares the arts of music and poetry:

> A minstrel once said to Khusraw, "O treasure of words,
> Is the science of music nobler than the art of poetry?
> Since the former is a science that cannot be penned precisely,
> And the latter is an art that exists on paper and pen."
> I answered him, "I am an expert in both fields.
> It is fitting that I weigh them on a scale.
> I composed poetry that came out to be three books,
> They are three books of the science of music, if you can
>   believe it.
> I will tell you the difference between the two correctly,
> If someone who is knowledgeable about them can judge.
> Imagine poetry to be a science that is complete in itself,
> Indeed, it needs no notes nor the voice of a minstrel.
> If someone sings a poem in a low or high tone, it's fine,
> There is no harm done to the meaning or the words.
> If a minstrel just utters some sounds as a song,
> Without words it will be meaningless and worthless.
> Look at the flute player who has a voice and the song of his
>   flute,
> He is compelled to have another person for the words (*qawl*).
> In this respect, singer and listener are both necessary;
> For poetry, a discerning patron is necessary.
> Consider poetry to be a bride and song her ornament,
> There is no harm if a beautiful bride is without ornament."

Each art enhances the other but one is demonstrably more powerful and effective than the other. Music is essential in appreciating and understanding the rhythm and meters of Persian lyric poetry. Just as there is an apocryphal anecdote about Rumi passing through the bazaar of the goldsmiths and being inspired by the rhythmic sound of their tools to compose a poem, so there is one about Amir Khusraw replicating the sound of the cotton carder's bow in a verse.

References to music and musical instruments abound in Amir Khusraw's poetry, but this is not surprising, since Persian poets used imagery from a broad range of subjects in their poems. However, the details he provides demonstrate that he had technical knowledge of the musical arts. Music was an essential component of medieval Persianate courtly culture, and as was seen above in the vignette on Sultan Jalaluddin's court, Amir Khusraw's poems were put to music and performed in his own time. It would not be incorrect to assume that he may even have played an active role in putting his lyric poetry to music.

In the *masnavi Hasht bihisht*, which was part of his quintet, Amir Khusraw altered Nizami's original frame story by having his female protagonist Dilaram become adept at all kinds of music arts instead of achieving physical prowess to impress the king, Bahram Gur. Given all the circumstantial evidence, it is regrettable that there are no separate theoretical writings on music by Amir Khusraw, although they were believed at one time to exist. In *Nuh sipihr*, he claims that foreign musicians visiting India have introduced new features to Indian music but have not added anything to the basic principles. He says that the sound of Indian music captivates the wild deer, even in the face of the hunter's arrow: it is pierced and dies, killed not by the arrow but by the music. The second section of *I'jaz-i Khusravi*, the miscellany of epistles and prose pieces, is devoted to musical topics. Here he describes various musical instruments and mentions the accomplished musicians of his day, and describes the arrival of a group of musicians from Central Asia who competed with Indian artistes. He also mentions a lady by the name of Turmati Khatun who was an accomplished musician in charge of the Indian and Persian court musicians.

One of the many apocryphal stories about Amir Khusraw describes his victory in a contest with a famous Indian musician, Gopal, and his wresting of the title *nayak* for himself. It is also clear that Amir Khusraw was familiar with both the Indian and Persian musical systems of his day. The exact nature of his experiments with combining the *ragas* of Indian music with the *maqam* and *pardah* system of Arabic and Persian music cannot be ascertained. He is said to have introduced variations of melody and tempo and come up with over a dozen new modes in Indian music, some of which, such as *sazgiri*, *shahanah*, and *zilaf*, are still known today. The introduction of the *khayal* genre of music, which is the main vocal form performed today, is often attributed to Amir Khusraw or to the fifteenth-century Sultan Husayn Sharqi of Jaunpur. Another type of composition that he authored is the *taranah* (song), an onomatopoeic string of meaningless syllables interspersed with other bits of poetic lines and sung in any *raga*. With so many attributions to his name, perhaps it is safe to use the term current among musicologists, *Khusravi* style, to describe compositions that may have been influenced by Amir Khusraw or whose core can be traced to him. His greatest innovations are said to be the instruments *sitar* and *tabla*, now an essential part of Hindustani music, but there is no historical basis to the claim.

Amir Khusraw's connections to music continue to be a dynamic part of the living traditions of not only north Indian classical music but also the now universally popular form of qawwali. Music is an essential component of *qawwali*, which is the ecstatic and hypnotic performance of sufi verses, often accompanied by dance. The use of the term *qawwali* equally signifies the lyrics of the poems sung, the singing, and the whole presentation itself. The word is derived from the Arabic *qawl* (utterance, speech) and the form is actually a mixture of the Arabic *qawl* and the Persian *ghazal*. Listening to music (*sama'*) by sufis as part of their spiritual exercises has been a controversial topic throughout history, but the Chishtis were and are particularly inclined to it, and the art of *qawwali* has been fostered at their shrine complexes in such places as Delhi, Ajmer, Lucknow, and Lahore. The invention of this form of dance music and the training of the first generation of singers (*qawwal bachche*) is often ascribed to Amir Khusraw. It is likely that some form of *qawwali* formed part of the devotional practices of sufis before Amir Khusraw. In its present state, it was a uniquely South Asian development that emerged from the universal sufi practice of dance music and over time has taken on distinct styles according to region and schools of music. It is a constantly evolving form and the earliest recordings of *qawwali* from the turn of the last century are different from the current style of performance, but the core has always been Amir Khusraw's poetry.

Dance is present but is not the primary part of the Chishti rituals, unlike that of the Mevlevi sufis in Turkey. There are strict rules regarding the participation of sufis and lay people, as was true in the poet's time too:

> Amir Khusraw may have been the shaykh's dearest human companion, yet by the high standards that Nizam al-Din set for himself and for his most intimate disciples, the great poet could not be a soul brother of the great saint. The unbridged gulf between them is evoked in a graphic anecdote from *Siyar al-awliya'*:
> Once at a musical gathering presided over by the shaykh, Amir Khusraw threw up his hands in ecstasy and began to dance, as was common to Sufis while hearing religious verses

sung. Shaykh Nizam ad-Din summoned Khusraw to him
saying, "You are connected with this world; you are not
permitted to raise your hands when dancing." Amir Khusraw
brought down his hands, closed his fists and went on dancing.
(Ernst and Lawrence, 2002: 76–7)

This is a useful clue in understanding Amir Khusraw's position
in two separate worlds, material and spiritual, that rarely inter-
sected. He was an intimate of the sufi master but his courtly
connections limited his full participation in the practices of the
other mystics.

Qawwali provides the form in which Amir Khusraw's poetry
in Hindavi and Persian is still known and performed in a live
context that is completely removed from the written and illustrated tradition of his writings that is part of the culture of reading. As literary texts, lyrics sung in *qawwali* are intertextual and
combine Amir Khusraw's poems with occasional Arabic quotations and lines of Persian sufi poetry. The repertoire of *qawwali*
is dynamic and now accommodates all kinds of Persian, Urdu,
Hindi, and Panjabi verses, as seen in a recent publication by the
qawwal Meraj Ahmed Nizami. Thus, the language of *qawwali*
appeals to Muslim as well as non-Muslim South Asians, since
the poet often expresses his devotion for the Prophet
Muhammad, Imam 'Ali, or Nizamuddin Awliya in terms that
are also found in Hindu devotional contexts.

HINDAVI POETRY

The use of a vernacular register of poetry in Hindavi, a word
that is usually used to designate the language of the Delhi region,
or sometimes as a general term for any Indian language, may
have started before Amir Khusraw, but it became increasingly
common from his time onwards. With all the writing in Persian

that was taking place too, there was a parallel movement to produce literature in vernacular languages so as to make works more accessible to those who were not literate or who did not participate in the Persian courtly tradition. Both sufis and Hindu poets of the *bhakti* (devotional) movement used local languages to free themselves of traditional constraints. Literature produced at royal courts was meant only for the elite, but this elite was spread over the entire Persian world. By contrast, the works found in sufi *khanaqah*s had a more local audience, but socially it was more broadly based audience.

The following is one of the best known of Amir Khusraw's *ghazal*s, especially since it is macaronic, in Persian and Hindavi (the italicized parts are in Hindavi):

> Don't be heedless of my abject state, *He rolls his eyes, he makes excuses,*
> For I cannot bear this separation, *Why doesn't he take and embrace me?*
> The nights of separation are long like tresses, and the days of union short like life,
> *Girlfriend, if I don't see my beloved, how can I get through the dark nights?*
> All at once, two spell-binding eyes ruined my heart's composure a hundred times,
> *Who cares enough to carry my words to my beloved?*
> Like a burning candle, like a dazed atom, always crying, for the love of that moon,
> *No sleep for the eyes, no rest for the limbs, he doesn't come, he doesn't send letters.*
> For the sake of the day of union with my beloved who deceived me, Khusraw,
> *I will keep myself prepared until I can go to my beloved's abode.*

This is a complex poem consisting of dual voices, languages, and genders. Interestingly, in one sung version the male singer sings the Persian and the female singer the Hindavi. The poetics of separation exist in both languages and even though the two traditions are independent, here the words of the male poet/ lover and the pining female beloved complement each other. Due to the mixed nature of its languages, not surprisingly, this poem is not found in any of the poet's *divan*s and is not documented until the eighteenth century. It may not have been Amir Khusraw's poem at all but it has survived in an oral context and is in complete harmony with the spirit of his poetry.

In Amir Khusraw's Hindavi poetry, his *pir* is called the *jag ujiyaro* (world illuminator) and *maharaj* (emperor) along with a number of other epithets that make this a common language of devotion for practitioners of all faiths. The device of using a female voice to express her longing for a lover is characteristic of Indic poetry and here is used expertly by the poet to be as inclusive as possible. In a well-known *qawwali*, Amir Khusraw is the bride to the groom Nizamuddin in a symbolic union of the master and disciple, with other Chishti elders invoked too:

I am sold on your beautiful face, Nizam,
I am sold on your beautiful face.
Of all the girls' veils, mine is most soiled.
The women look at me and laugh, Nizam ...
This spring, dye my veil afresh,
Preserve my honor, beloved Nizam,
For the sake of Baba Ganj-e Shakar,
Preserve my honor, Nizam ...
Qutub and Farid have come in the groom's procession,
Khusro is the bride, Nizam ...
Some women fight with the mother-in-law, some with the
    sister-in-law,
But my hopes are set on you, Nizam ...
I am sold on your beautiful face. (Kidwai, 2000: 129–30)

In all the Hindavi poetic forms, gender plays an important role because it allows the poet to adopt a different persona and express his feelings through a female voice. In contrast, this remains a moot point in his Persian poems where there is no grammatical gender and the beauty of the work, to some extent, relies on sexual ambiguity.

Such poems of Amir Khusraw are virtual folksongs, though sung in a classical mode, with borrowings from the landscape of Indian culture, as in this poem written as if by a typical village woman who goes to fetch water from the well:

> The path to the well is hard –
> It's hard to go fill my pot with that wine.
> When I went to fill my pot with water
> It got broken in the mad rush,
> The path to the well is hard.
> Khusro has given himself to Nizam –
> Protect my honor, keep me veiled,
> The path to the well is hard. (Kidwai, 2000: 129)

The arduous journey to the well symbolizes the mystical path on which love is the main provision for the traveler. The flirtatious loveplay in these poems is also a common feature of devotional songs about the Hindu deity Krishna and the *gopi*s who complain about being teased incessantly by the divine lover.

Similarly in another song, Nizamuddin Awliya asks the Chishti sufis to come out in their ecstatic state and join the celebrations of the Hindu spring festival of Holi, which is an occasion for great revelry and playfulness. True to their acceptance of local practices, Chishtis also celebrate another Indian folk spring festival, *basant*. According to popular belief, the genesis of their participation in this festival is found in an event from Amir Khusraw's life. One day, he saw some Hindu women singing and carrying mustard flowers to offer to their deity on the religious festival of

basant panchmi. In order to cheer up Nizamuddin Awliya, who
was depressed about his nephew's death, Amir Khusraw dressed
up like a Hindu woman and proceeded towards his *pir* singing the
song he had heard. This brought a smile to Nizamuddin Awliya's
face and the festival became a major celebration, its whole ritual
part of the Chishti tradition. There are also songs said to have been
composed by Amir Khusraw especially for the occasion of *basant*.

Whether Amir Khusraw really wrote poetry in a vernacular
language and if so, whether the corpus of literature in Hindavi
ascribed to him is really his work, are difficult questions from a
textual and historical point of view. As he himself says:

> I am a parrot of India if you ask me candidly,
> Ask me in Hindavi so that I can answer you correctly.

This verse has been taken to signify his pride in primarily being
a poet in his mother tongue, but is clearly no indication of what
he actually composed in this language. Elsewhere, he reiterates
this opinion, this time downplaying his ability to compose
Arabic verse:

> I am a Turk of Hindustan, I answer in Hindavi,
> I don't have Egyptian sugar to speak Arabic.

Sugar refers to the poet's words that have the quality of sweetness. Such a display of self-deprecation appears to be merely a
poetic stance and not a statement regarding a regular practice.

The entire body of Hindavi works attributed to Amir
Khusraw, all in verse form, is based on oral tradition and to a
large extent has been mixed up with other folksongs and
poems. The written tradition of these works can only be traced
back to the eighteenth and nineteenth centuries, by which time
historical circumstances had made it imperative to invent a
Hindavi body of poetry authored by Amir Khusraw. The spoken
language that was Hindavi was constantly changing, and the

songs in their current state probably represent the last recorded recension of these works. Thus the original of Hindavi poems and songs may well have been by Amir Khusraw, but no definitive text can be prepared on the basis of the multiple versions that abound today. As with other great medieval poets, minor poets would add their own poems to that of the master's *oeuvre* in order to derive prestige by association with them. However, since nobody doubts the fact that Amir Khusraw wrote in Hindavi and the question of authenticity is moot, the point is to focus on the place of these texts in today's society.

In addition to the devotional songs about Nizamuddin Awliya discussed above, Amir Khusraw's authorship is attached to women's folksongs sung at weddings, riddles, and any genre of Hindavi poetry that involves *double entendre* or wordplay. The fact that the poet was so fond of puns and enjoyed switching language codes makes a strong case for his having authored this body of literature. In addition to Persian riddles (*chistan*), there is a category (*dosukhane*) where the question is asked in two languages while the answer is a homonym that answers both questions:

> *Kuh chih midarad?* (Persian) *Musafir ko kya chahiye?*
> (Hindi/Urdu)
> What does the mountain have? What does a traveler want?
> *Sang*
> Stone/Companionship

The riddle can take another form:

> I saw a wondrous child in the land of Hindustan,
> His skin covered his hair, and his hair his bones!
> Answer: Mango

There are innumerable riddles like these in the *Khusravi* mode.

Another genre of poetry that is drawn upon in folk poetry is the *shahrashub,* which in Persian is a flirtatious exchange between the poet and a boy who is engaged in a particular trade or task. The earliest of these were written in the form of quatrains, and in Amir Khusraw's poems there is often a woman in place of a boy. This is one of his "purely" Persian poems:

> I saw a mendicant boy sitting in the dust,
> His face was beautiful like that of Layla, but his head downcast
>   like Majnun,
> Indeed, his beauty was enhanced by the dust,
> For a mirror becomes brighter when polished with dust.

In some of these, the first three lines are Persian, while the last is mixed Persian–Hindavi. In the following quatrain, the last line uttered by the woman is a pun, i.e., it can be read both as a Persian sentence or a Hindavi one:

> I went for a stroll by a stream
> And saw a Hindu woman on the water's edge,
> I asked, "Pretty one, what is the price of your hair?"
> She cried out, "Every hair a pearl/Get lost, you lout!"

The enduring presence of this genre of poetry in the daily lives of South Asians exists in an advertisement for yogurt from a magazine published in Lahore that depicts a traditional female yogurt-seller and Amir Khusraw as he is commonly envisaged, with the text of his poem about her in Persian/Hindavi and in an Urdu translation.

Amir Khusraw's playful side can also be seen in a category of Hindavi poetry (*mukarni*) of a bawdy nature in the form of two female friends conversing about the lover of one of them, which again relies on witty wordplay:

> "Once a year he comes to my town,
> With his mouth on my mouth, he feeds me juices,

I spend much money on him."
"Who, girlfriend, your man?" "No, girlfriend, a mango."

There are a number of such *mukarni*s attributed to Amir Khusraw but whose language and style vary so considerably that they cannot have been authored by one individual. All these forms of folk poetry are so common and unquestionably considered to be the work of the great poet that the issue is no longer one of establishing the authenticity of these texts but of the symbolic attribution of linguistically significant utterances that are part of a living and dynamic culture.

In the same way that Amir Khusraw has been crowned as the father of Indo-Persian poetry, so he has been invoked as the founder of the Urdu language in order to enhance the prestige of the language, which is relatively new in South Asia, but related to Hindavi and Persian. Thus, works like the once popular *Tale of the Four Dervishes*, which is extant in Urdu translations, is falsely attributed to Amir Khusraw, as is the Persian–Hindi dictionary *Khaliq bari*, which is now believed to have been written in the seventeenth century by one Ziyauddin Khusraw. Both of these texts were used by generations of Indians and Europeans in colonial India to learn Persian. Sa'di, the famous poet of Shiraz, who was mentioned above as supposedly having been invited to Multan by Amir Khusraw's patron in the 1280s, is also said to have come to India to learn Urdu, a language that did not exist at that time, from the Indian poet! However, forging such literary connections with iconic figures from the past, just like inventing a meeting between two famous personages who lived close to each other in history, is a symbolic moment in the history of many cultures. The fact remains that Amir Khusraw's Hindavi, or Hindi, is the precursor of the modern languages Urdu and Hindi.

Given the prestige attached to his persona as a Hindavi poet, Amir Khusraw was accorded a major role in the first attempt to write a history of Urdu literature using western critical methods by the poet and critic Muhammad Husain Azad (d. 1910). In his *Ab-i hayat* (Water of Life), which appeared in 1881, Azad makes various claims about Amir Khusraw's literary innovations and supplies anecdotes to support the popular view of the poet. For this author writing at the end of the classical period and the beginning of modernity of Urdu, Amir Khusraw was still part of a living culture:

> In Delhi, or rather in a number of the cities of India, the custom is that at the height of the rainy season, most women have stakes driven into the ground – or if there's a tree, they use that – and have a swing put up. They gather together and swing, and sing songs, and enjoy themselves. There will scarcely be a single woman among them who doesn't sing this song: "My beloved said he would come, / My lord has not come, / Alas, my beloved said he would come, / He said he would come, would come, / He has not come for a whole twelve months, / Alas, my beloved said he would come", and so on. This song too is by Amir Khusrau, and it is in the Barva *rag* that he invented. Bravo! – what tongues those people had, that whatever fell from their lips pleased the whole world, and engraved itself on the heart of the age! Composers have composed thousands of songs, singers have sung them; they are here today, and forgotten tomorrow. Six hundred years have passed. His songs are alive even today, and give brightness to every rainy season. If this marvelous acceptance is not an innate, divine gift, then what is it?

This is a rare glimpse into the cultural practices of nineteenth-century women in north India. Azad goes on to narrate an anecdote that is reminiscent of Amir Khusraw's being tested as a composer of poetry when he was still a child:

At a well, four female water-carriers were drawing water.
Amir Khusrau, walking along the road, felt thirsty. Going to
the well, he asked one of the women for water. One of them
recognized him. She said to the others, "Look, this is Khusrau
himself." They asked, "Are you the Khusrau whose songs
everybody sings, and whose riddles and *mukarni*s and
misjoinders everybody listens to?" He said, "Yes!" At this,
one of them said, "Compose something about rice pudding
for me." The second named a spinning wheel, the third a
drum, the fourth a dog. He said, "I'm dying of thirst. First
give me some water to drink." They said, "Until you compose
what we said, we won't give you any water." He quickly
composed this misjoinder: " 'I cooked rice pudding with
effort, I burned the spinning wheel; a dog came and ate it up
– you sit and play the drum!' Come on, give me some water!"

Azad also mentions Amir Khusraw's musical inventions, and
goes on to relate another anecdote that highlights the poet's
interest in wordplay, music, and folk culture:

A wandering faqir came as a guest to Sultan-ji Sahib
[Nizamuddin Awliya]'s place. In the evening, he sat at the
dining-cloth. After eating, they began to talk. The traveler
spread out so many reams of talk that much of the night
passed, and it just didn't end. Sultan-ji Sahib yawned
somewhat, and stretched himself a bit, but that simple-
minded person didn't understand at all. Sultan-ji Sahib,
fearing to hurt the feelings of a guest, could say nothing;
having no choice, he had to stay seated. Amir Khusrau too was
present, but he couldn't speak up. Then the midnight gong
was struck, and at that time Sultan-ji said, "Khusrau, what
hour has struck?" He petitioned, "It's the midnight gong."
Sultanj-ji asked, "What voice can be heard in it?" He said, "I
understand it to say: 'You ate bread – go home. You ate bread
– go home. Go home – go home. / You ate bread – go home. I
haven't mortgaged the house to you. Go home – go home.' "

Think of how the sounds move and stop, and how they
express each and every stroke of the gong, and what effect
this had. (Azad, 2001: 98–9)

It is in charming anecdotes like these that the irresistible
personality of Amir Khusraw comes alive for speakers of Hindi
and Urdu today and continues to have a hold in their collective
cultural imagination. The synthesis between Persian and Indian
poetics that can be seen in some of Amir Khusraw's writings
would occur again, and in a more sustained and formal manner,
among the Dakhni poets of the sixteenth and seventeenth centuries in southern India. Unfortunately, such literary innovations are considered non-canonical in retrospect by upholders
of the high traditions.

DESCRIBING INDIA

The first Muslim to write about India in a systematic and
scientific manner was Abu Rayhan al-Biruni (d. 1048), who
had accompanied the Ghaznavid sultan Mahmud to India
and written his remarkable work *Kitab al-Hind* as a result
of first-hand observation of the peoples and cultural practices
of the land. Although al-Biruni had studied Sanskrit in order to
be able to read Hindu texts, his viewpoint was that of an
outsider. From an inside point of view, during the Mughal
times, the fourth section of Abu al-Fazl's (d. 1602) monumental
A'in-i Akbari (Institutes of Akbar) would also be a tremendous
contribution to Muslim knowledge about India. But no other
author in Persian has written so widely and in such an
imaginative way about India as Amir Khusraw. Tidbits of
information from his works, be they in poetry or prose, have
done much to enhance our knowledge about life in thirteenth-
and fourteenth-century India. However, it should be kept

in mind that Amir Khusraw is not engaged in a detached scholarly study of India such as al-Biruni's, and some of his fanciful ideas must be understood in the context of his creative endeavor and the particular genre into which a work falls.

The narrative work *Nuh sipihr* has an entire section providing encyclopedic information on different aspects of Indian culture and the poet's arguments for his belief in the superiority of India in the Islamic world. Amir Khusraw constructs several fanciful arguments to prove that India is akin to paradise: it is the land to which Adam first came after being expelled from paradise, according to one Islamic tradition; the peacock, the bird of paradise, is indigenous to the place; the climate is pleasant and moderate, he says, referring to a saying (*hadith*) by the Prophet Muhammad that he enjoyed the cool breeze that wafted from India; and last, but not least, India is superior because his patron lives there. To settle the matter, he boasts that this is the land where a great poet like himself resides! The abundance of the flora and fauna, fruits like mangoes and bananas, spices like cardamom and cloves, and the quintessentially Indian betel-leaf (*pan*) add to the virtues of this land. He goes on to describe the religion and learning of the Brahmans in a lively and anecdotal style. Moving to the area of world civilization, the game of chess and the book of stories *Kalila wa Dimna* both originated in India.

This is followed by a claim that he has learned several languages, and the poet propounds a fascinating discourse on the languages of the world:

> Arabic has fixed rules of grammar and syntax so that people do not make errors in it. These are not just mechanical rules but [are] there for reciting the *Qur'an* and studying the sciences. Scholars have written a grammar and dictionary for Turkish too, for in some parts of the world it is the official

language and is used for military and administrative purposes.
But nobody learns Turkish or Greek or Dari [Persian] in order
to acquire knowledge. Only Arabic is widespread and used
worldwide. Arabic has ennobled everyone and users of Arabic
are not marginalized. For all the sweetness of the Persians, no
rhetorician has established a grammar for it. I could do it; it is
my wish to correct this situation but Persian speakers have no
need for it. Since I do not see anyone *not* using Dari, my
efforts would be futile ... Three languages in this world are
valued like pearls. Each of these three has originated from a
fixed place but are used throughout the world. First is Arabic,
which originated among the Arabs but adorned the lips of the
whole world, in the east and west, among scholars and
learned men ... Next comes Persian of the Persians, which
originated in Shiraz. Persian spread from there, becoming
the banner of the world and the moonlike landmark of every
city. Then comes Turkish of the Turks of various tribes. It
originated in the Qipchaq and Yamaq plains and spread to
other countries, like the salt of India. There are other choice
languages but none bright like these ... It is the ancient
custom that the language of the rulers becomes widespread in
the world. For example, Persian was commonly used in
Baghdad, and when the caliphs established themselves there,
the Persians rose to power and influenced the manners of the
Arabs. The city that the Arabs call Baghdad was once called
the Garden of Justice (*Baghchah-e dad*). Turkish too gained
popularity when the Turkish rulers conquered the world, and
it began to be spoken in the world. India followed this pattern
in speech: Hindavi was the language from old times; when the
Ghurids and Turks arrived, Persian began to be used and
every high and low person learnt it ... As I belong to India,
it is only fitting that I talk about it. There is a different,
original language in every region of this land. Sindi, Lahori,
Kashmiri, Kibar, Dhaur Samundari, Tilangi, Gujar, Ma'bari,
Gauri, the languages of Bangalah, Avadh, Delhi and its

environs, all these are Hindavi, i.e., Indian languages, current
since the olden days and commonly used for all kinds of
speech. There is yet another language that is favored by all
the Brahmans. It is known as Sanskrit since ancient times;
common people do not know it, only the Brahmans do,
but one single Brahman cannot comprehend its limits. Like
Arabic, Sanskrit has a grammar, rules of syntax, and a
literature ... Sanskrit is a pearl; it may be inferior to Arabic
but is superior to Dari ... If I knew it well I would praise my
sultan in it also.

The above discussion provides a useful insight into the mapping
of the languages of the world from a medieval Indian point
of view, and a remarkably open-minded one too. In Amir
Khusraw's worldview, the three classical languages of Islam,
Arabic, Persian, and Turkish, complement the host of Indian
languages, and each has its specific sphere of usage, either as a
language of learning, administration, literature, or communi-
cation. It seems that Turkish was spoken by an elite group in
India but no literature in it was produced, even by the poet.
Persian was more current in India for administrative and literary purposes, but it did not seem to be in competition with any
other major language. Interestingly, the use of the desgination
"Persian" refers to the Persian language of Iran and "Dari" as the
more literary form of it that was widely used in Central and
South Asia. Scholars have identified the Indian languages that
Amir Khusraw mentions, a list that gives a good sense of the
situation of vernacular languages at this time.

Elsewhere, in the introduction to his third *divan*, he includes
a similar discussion about languages, where he states that unlike
Hindavi, which changes every hundred miles, the Persian of
India, i.e., Dari, is standard from the river Indus to the Indian
Ocean and does not have dialect variants as in Iran. "What is

amusing," he declares, "is that we [Indians] have composed
poetry in the languages of all people [of the world] but no one
has composed poetry in our language."

In the next section, a compendium of the different kinds
of birds and animals found in India is given. The next part
deals with the marvels and wonders of India, especially the
supernatural powers of the Hindu yogis. This kind of
writing about strange facts in exotic lands is in the tradition
of a well-established genre of Arabic literature, where India
always finds a substantial space. Towards the end of the
India section of the work, he comments on the intelligence
of the inhabitants of the country and the openness of the
culture:

> If a Khurasani, Greek or Arab comes here,
> He will not face any problems.
> For they will treat him kindly, as their own,
> Making him feel at ease and happy.
> And if they jest with him,
> They do so laughingly, like flowers.

It is remarkable that this perception of India as an open society,
which seems quite modern in some ways, was already formed
in the early fourteenth century.

In this encyclopedic section on India in his work, Amir
Khusraw is attempting to put forward an alternative worldview, one that is Indocentric and that challenges existing ideas
about the classification of civilizations in the world of Islam. In
this new worldview, Islam has the central place but there is
room for all the complexities of Indian cultural traditions.
Amir Khusraw's hyperbolic arguments must be seen as rhetorical exercises intended to impress his audience. What he is trying to do in this work is to instill a sense of pride in Indians,
Muslims in particular, and to give them a distinct culture

within the context of a larger Islamic civilization, just as the Arabs and Persians had their own culture from early Islamic times. He sincerely believes that the *shari'at* attained perfection in India and that it was the ideal place for the flowering of Muslim civilization.

THE POET IN OUR TIME

Amir Khusraw lived in politically unstable times and witnessed the highest and lowest points in the history of the Delhi Sultanate. As someone who maintained his position throughout this and was able to negotiate the rival worlds of the royal and sufi courts, he provided a model for subsequent generations of Indians. His popularity in Persian literature was to increase as time went on. In fact, in the sixteenth century an eminent Iranian émigré at the Mughal court, Hakim Abu al-Fath Gilani, declared that Amir Khusraw was the only worthy poet of Persian in India. But notwithstanding continuing interest in the poet, the state of academic research on Amir Khusraw is paradoxical in that despite the existence of a vast body of secondary writings on him as a poet and sufi, there is little new or interesting work on his actual writing. A large part of his poetry remains unpublished or unavailable in critical editions, and awaits the attention of scholars.

The poet has fared much better in the public sphere. At the celebration of the '*urs* of both Amir Khusraw and Nizamuddin Awliya at the tomb complex (*dargah*) in Delhi, performers from far-flung regions of South Asia, such as Bangladesh, Sindh, Panjab, and the Deccan, come together to commemorate the death of the poet and celebrate the mystical marriage, signified by the word '*urs*, of the poet with God and re-enact the love between him and his beloved guide. Meraj Ahmed Nizami is the

well-loved and admired senior *qawwal* there, one of the descen-
dants of the first generation of *qawwal bachche*, as are other
artistes in the musical schools (*gharana*) of Delhi, Agra,
Gwalior, and Rampur. Numerous performers, such as Nusrat
Fateh Ali Khan and the Sabri brothers of Pakistan, and Jafar
Husain and Mohammad Ahmad Warsi of Uttar Pradesh, India,
have been instrumental in making *qawwali* part of world music.
Hamsar Hayat is one of the youngest performers of the *qawwal
bachche* to have arrived on the international scene recently. In
March 2002, Muzaffar Ali organized the Festival of Amir
Khusraw in Delhi, at which, in a collaborative effort, the
Pakistani singer Abida Parveen and Tunisian singer Lotfi
Bouchnak, accompanied by other performers from Iran,
presented the traditional repertoire in a new context. This
promises to be an annual cultural event that will connect an
earlier phase of the history of Delhi to the present world. The
dargah of Nizamuddin Awliya is a familiar one in the landscape
of Delhi, where Muslim devotees mingle with local Hindus and
Sikhs, foreign tourists, and aficionados of *qawwali*.

Amir Khusraw's Hindavi and Persian poems are also sung
in secular contexts. The Afghan classical performer Ustad
Mohammad Sarahang, who was both the court musician of
King Zahir and professor of music at Kabul University, has rendered the poet's Persian *ghazals* in a style that is characteristic
of the Kabul school of classical music with its roots in India. A
range of artistes from the melodious *ghazal* singer Iqbal Bano to
popular singers associated with Bollywood such as Mukesh and
Asha Bhosle have sung the Persian lyrics of Amir Khusraw, con-
tributing new dimensions to the enjoyment of the poems.

The seven-hundredth anniversary of the poet was celebrated with great fanfare in India, Pakistan, Afghanistan, and
the Soviet Union in 1975, and a number of publications
appeared in connection with the event. In 1997, Yousuf Saeed

and Iffat Fatima in Delhi made a four-part documentary in Hindi for the network television Doordarshan, *Bujh sake to bujh* (Guess If You Can), on the different aspects of the poet's life. Yousuf Saeed also maintains a useful and interesting website on the poet (www.alif-india.com) that shows the tenderness and reverence with which people still regard Amir Khusraw. The seven hundred and fiftieth anniversary of the poet's birth was celebrated on 9 August 2003 in New Delhi at an official event. In recent years the Chishti festival of *basant,* which has always been celebrated at the Nizamuddin *dargah* in Delhi since the poet's lifetime, has been publicized by cultural experts and has become a major event symbolizing communal harmony by bringing together groups of people from different spheres of life.

Amir Khusraw, through the legacy of his Persian writings and contributions to music and folklore, is uniquely positioned to be of relevance to today's world. With the existence of so many, often overlapping, identities, such as Muslim and Hindu, South Asian, Persian, scholar, and sufi, combined with a renewed interest in pre-modern forms of life that can be accessed only through a knowledge of languages and texts, for which Persian and Hindavi loom large on the horizon, he takes on a particular importance. Though he was a Muslim poet who functioned in an Islamic environment, he has touched the lives of many beyond his community, not only in his lifetime, but down to our time, as people in South Asia and outside have received his *oeuvre* and responded to his message. Going back to the world that he lived in, there is another enlightening anecdote about that great patron saint of Delhi, Nizamuddin Awliya, about whom Hasan writes:

> A disciple of the master's arrived and brought a Hindu friend with him. He introduced him by saying, "This is my brother." When he had greeted both of them, the master – may God remember him with favor – asked that disciple: "And does

this brother of yours have any inclination towards Islam?" "It is to this end," replied the disciple, "that I have brought him to the master, that by the blessing of your gaze he might become a Muslim." The master – may God remember him with favor – became teary-eyed. "You can talk to this people as much as you want," he observed, "and no one's heart will be changed, but if you find the company of a righteous person, then it may be hoped that by the blessing of his company the other will become a Muslim." (Hasan Sijzi, 1992: 285–6)

This was the message that Nizamuddin Awliya as a sufi, and Amir Khusraw as a littérateur, sought to impart to the people they came into contact with, and this is what is appealing about their lives and writings for us today. The historical and cultural context that must be understood in order to enter the complex world that they inhabited makes the endeavor all the more interesting. Whether it is through Persian court poetry, qawwali or the discourses of a sufi pir, that world is not as inaccessible as it may seem.

In conclusion, we can return to the question of the vast body of Amir Khusraw's works and the enigma of his personality. He has too many personae to be captured under one label, although he was foremost a poet, but perhaps we can turn to his favorite rhetorical device, iham, to understand the complexities we see in his personality and works. He says, "[My] talent has established iham as clearer than a mirror, for in a mirror more than one image does not appear from an object. But this is a mirror that when you look into it, seven true and clear images will appear."

BIOGRAPHICAL ACCOUNT
OF AMIR KHUSRAW
FROM AMIR KHURD'S
SIYAR AL-AWLIYA

M uhammad ibn Mubarak Kirmani Amir Khurd (d. 1369) was a disciple of Nizamuddin Awliya and his successor Nasiruddin Mahmud Chiragh-i Dehli. He wrote a hybrid text, part biographical dictionary and part *malfuzat*, called *Siyar al-awliya* (Biography of Saints). This book is in ten chapters and is a rich source for the lives and practices of the early sufi masters. The following is a translation of his account of Amir Khusraw's life,[1] from an overtly Chishti point of view, but it is the earliest of all biographies and from the pen of an individual who knew Amir Khusraw personally. This text is also representative of medieval Persian works of this genre and illustrates the various tropes and literary devices utilized in the composition of a hagiographical account.

---

1. Amir Khurd, *Siyar al-awliyā' dar ahvāl va malfūzāt-i mashāyikh-i Chisht*, ed. Muhammad Arshad Quraishi (Islamabad: Markaz-i Tahqīqāt-i Fārsī Īrān va Pākistān, 1978), 311–15.

The sultan of poets, proven among scholars, the poet Amir Khusraw – may God have mercy on him, who had surpassed the ancients and contemporaries in learning, had a pure mind. The way of sufis was manifest in his appearance and character, and although he was affiliated with kings, he was among those about whom it has been said, "Be prepared for service to the sultan *and* be a sufi."

The writer of these words heard from his own father – may God have mercy on him, that on the day that Amir Khusraw was born, in the neighboring house of his father Amir Lachin, there was a madman with a natural gift, and Amir Khusraw's father wrapped Amir Khusraw in swaddling clothes and took him before the madman. The madman said, "You have brought someone who will be two steps ahead of [the poet] Khaqani."

Thus when he became an adult, he was honored by the affection of Sultan al-Mashayikh [Nizamuddin Awliya], singled out for all kinds of favors and kindnesses and held in special regard. In those days, Sultan al-Mashayikh used to live in the house of Ravat-i 'Arz, the maternal grandfather of Amir Khusraw, near the Manda bridge gate. At that time, Amir Khusraw had begun to compose poetry. Every poem that he wrote he presented to Sultan al-Mashayikh, until one day Sultan al-Mashayikh said, "Compose in the style of the Isfahanis, i.e. love poetry about tresses and moles." From that day on, Amir Khusraw – may God have mercy on him, became occupied with tresses and moles of beauties and described those lovely features masterfully. Afterwards, he presented his verses from first to last, along with Qazi Mu'izzuddin Pa'ichah, father of Rafi'uddin Pa'ichah, entirely to Sultan al-Mashayikh. He investigated the mysteries and symbolism of the poetry, and of all the poets achieved a high status before the kings.

He dedicated himself with such sincere devotion to his love for Sultan al-Mashayikh that he became the confidante of that great one. One day when he placed a poem praising Sultan al-Mashayikh before the Sultan al-Mashayikh, he was asked, "What do you desire?" Since he craved poetic words, he asked for the sweetness of language. The command came forth, "Bring that bowl of sugar from under the cot and sprinkle it over your head and eat some of it." Amir Khusraw did so and consequently the sweetness of his words captured the world from east to west and he became the pride of all the generations of poets. His request was granted until the end of his life at which time he had regrets that he had not asked for more. Libraries became filled with books written by him. When he would finish a book, he would present it to Sultan al-Mashayikh. Sultan al-Mashayikh used to take the book in his hand and say, "Let us recite the *fatiha*," and thus would hand it back to Amir Khusraw. If it happened that he opened it and glanced at a few lines, this too was for the benefit of Amir Khusraw so that he would not be deceived by the craft of poetry and would pursue a better line of work.

This great man had a fixed routine. Every night in his prayers he read the word of God in seven of thirty portions of the Qur'an. One day Sultan al-Mashayikh asked him, "Turk, what is the state of being occupied?" He replied humbly, "There are times at the end of the night when one is overcome by weeping," and Sultan al-Mashayikh said, "Praise be to God! Bit by bit it is becoming manifest." Sultan al-Mashayikh wrote several letters containing subtle points to Amir Khusraw in his auspicious script, the morals of which are recorded in this book. Amir Khusraw had full access to Sultan al-Mashayikh anytime he wanted, and he went before him and consulted him in all matters. If one of the senior disciples had a request, he would ask Amir Khusraw to present it, as has been written by Shaykh Nasiruddin.

The kindnesses of Sultan al-Mashayikh towards Amir Khusraw have been recorded. An example is the time when Sultan al-Mashayikh told him [Amir Khusraw], "I am weary of everyone, but I do not become weary of you." The second time he said, "I am weary of everyone, to the extent that I am weary of myself, but I do not become weary of you." When a man audaciously requested Sultan al-Mashayikh to show him just one favor of the many that were bestowed on Amir Khusraw, he did not reply in his presence but he told Amir Khusraw, "At that time, it crossed my mind that I should ask that man to show that same worthiness."

Once the Khvajah [Nizamuddin Awliya] said, "Repeat my prayer for your permanence is dependent upon my permanence. They must bury you next to me." These words were often repeated to Amir Khusraw and he said that it would happen thus, God Almighty willing. The servitude of the slave [Amir Khusraw] to the Khvajah is a pact of God, and whenever he strolls in paradise, may he have the slave next to him in paradise, God almighty willing.

Once the Khvajah saw in a dream that at the end of the Manda bridge, near the gate in front of the house of Najibuddin Mutavakkil, there was flowing water, extremely limpid and pure, and he was seated on a high place. It was an exhilarating moment. At such a moment it passed through my mind to ask God for blessings for you Amir Khusraw that are sought by us. I know that the prayer was answered and that state would appear in you, God almighty willing.

Amir Khusraw said: Once I heard from the auspicious tongue of the Khvajah, "Tonight I heard a voice in my head that Khusraw is not the name of a dervish, call Khusraw by the name of Muhammad the lowly. This command has come to me from the unseen and the prophet informed me that with this name he

is assured of eternal blessings, God the Bestower willing."
Khvajah called me Turk of God and many decorative and ornate
letters were written in his auspicious hand that referred to me
by this title. I have made a talisman of it so that it is with me
when I am buried.

> Before you, I am the one above everybody else,
> In the path of your love, I am the lowliest.

Khvajah summoned me. When I went before him he said, "I had a
dream, listen to it." Then he narrated it with his auspicious
tongue: On Friday night I saw in a dream that Shaykh Sadruddin
son of Shaykh al-Islam Bahauddin Zakariya – may God have
mercy on him, came before me. I came forward with full
humility; he himself showed such humility that it cannot be
described. Meanwhile I saw that you, Khusraw, appeared from
afar and came near us and began to express mystical views. In the
meantime, Salih the muezzin gave the call to prayer and I woke
up. When he described this dream, he said, "Look, what a rank
this is!" After that, poor me, I presented myself wailing and abject
saying, "What am I, a sweeper, to have that rank that after all is
given by you." At these words, the Khvajah began to sob in loud
tones; affected by him, I also began to sob. After that the Khvajah
asked for a special hat, with his own blessed hands he put it on my
head and said, "You must heed well the words of the Mashayikh."

Sultan al-Mashayikh recited the two verses out of the
extreme affection he had for Amir Khusraw:

> Khusraw has few peers in poetry and prose,
> His is the sovereignty of the kingdom of speech.
> That is our Khusraw, and not Nasir Khusraw,
> For God is the helper of our Khusraw.

Praise be to God, could there be a better moment than when on
the tongue of Hazrat Sultan al-Mashayikh – may God keep his
secret – there was praise of Amir Khusraw. Bravo to the perfect

grandeur of Amir Khusraw and the kindness and nurturance of Sultan al-Mashayikh – may God keep his secret.

I now return to writing about Amir Khusraw – may God have mercy on him. Once in Ghiyaspur, Amir Khusraw was invited to the house of this writer's father – may God have mercy on him. Sultan al-Mashayikh and the nobles of the city were present. Bahlul the *qawwal* sang this *ghazal* of Amir Hasan:

> Bravo Turk, who from his arched eyebrows
> Forms a bow, and shoots an arrow.
> How can every secret that exists inside the flute
> Find a place in the ear of the pretender?

In short, when they ended the *sama'* Amir Khusraw began his own *ghazal*. After he read the first couplet, he became silent and began a *ghazal* of Shaykh Sa'di:

> Your teacher taught you all the arts of flirtation and love,
> He taught you coquetry, censure, and cruelty.

He sang this *ghazal* in extremely moving tones. Afterwards they asked him, "What is the matter? Everytime you sing your own *ghazal*, you become silent." He said, "There are so many meanings in it that I get confused in trying to grasp them."

In conclusion, Amir Khusraw accompanied Sultan Ghiyasuddin Tughlaq to Lakhnawti. During his absence Sultan al-Mashayikh passed away. When he returned from that trip he blackened his face, tore his shirt, and rolling on the ground came towards the hovel of Sultan al-Mashayikh, with torn clothes, weeping eyes, and blood racing in his heart. Then he said, "O Muslims! Who am I to grieve for such a king, rather let me grieve for myself for after Sultan al-Mashayikh I will not have long to live." After that he lived for six months, then passed away. He was buried at the far end of the garden of Sultan al-Mashayikh – may God have mercy on him.

THE TALE OF THE TATAR PRINCESS GULNARI
Narrated on Tuesday in the Red Pavilion, from Amir Khusraw's Hasht Bihisht

Five young and talented friends
Set off from the city of Multan.   1

One of them was a prince,
Who from greatness had fallen upon hard times.   2

The second was a merchant's son,
Who had ample capital and even more merchandise.   3

The third was a skilled tunnel-digger,
Whose tool could loosen a mountain's base.   4

The fourth was a master carpenter,
Whose steel axe was able to split a hair.   5

The fifth was an excellent gardener,
Who wove tales with his flower arrangements.   6

The merchant's son, at all times,
Kindly took care of their expenses.   7

All friends who got on well,
They came to the limits of Kamru.[1]   8

In that fragrant land, their caravan
Passed by a city like paradise.   9

In its environs fresh as the spring
The caravan leader pitched the tents.   10

Those fine young men all in step,
Were strolling through the city,   11

Walking all around to view
The gardens, meadows and streams,   12

When in their activity, the sightseers
Came upon an old idol-temple.   13

It was a pavilion stretching tall
That could bewitch a thousand artists.   14

Artists of Mani's talent had sculpted
Its masterly images of stone.   15

Every figure was so beautiful that
A viewer would remain gazing at it.   16

The spectators approaching it
Were stupefied by the sight.   17

Of all the alluring forms,
Their gaze was fixed on one: 18

Which was incomparably beautiful and
Surpassed the others in craftsmanship.   19

As a signature of his work, *Kamrani* was
Written on its head by the artist.   20

1. Kamru or Kamrup, between Assam and Bengal, was known in legend
as a city of magicians and tantrics.

The moon-faced original of that idol
Lived in Kamru and her name was Kamrani.   21

In the language of the Hindus,
Kam means love and *rani* woman.[1]   22

Gazing at its beauty,
Their eyes were dazzled.   23

The eyes of the viewers were fixed,
As if they were portraits on a wall.   24

Rapture took over their minds as
Love rendered them restless.   25

Although no heart was untouched,
The prince especially became restless.   26

Until night's tresses veiled the day,
His eyes did not stray from that sight.   27

When night displayed the idol-temple
Of a dark sky with a hundred thousand idols,   28

The weary travelers besought him so that
They could return to their quarters.   29

Each person's heart was set on going home,
Except for the prince's, who had lost his.   30

He said, "I have lost control over myself!
Alas! The matter has gone out of hand.   31

This stone-hearted form has stolen my heart,
This stone has shattered my mirror.   32

1. In Persian, *kamrani* means "Success" or "Happiness" and in Hindi
"Lady Love."

From now on until my life ends,
My soul will be with this portrait.   33

Either I will lose myself in this figure
Or I will find the original."   34

All the friends were perplexed
By this confusing turn of events.   35

They counseled him but it was of no avail,
Whatever they said was useless.   36

When love is simmering in the heart,
Can advice be contained in the ear?   37

They all despaired of the outcome
And spent the night in that temple.   38

He, smitten by a stone, with a heavy heart,
Was like a doll that did not close its eyes.   39

When morning tore the world's curtain,
And in the manner of lovers rent its own clothes,   40

The lover remained devoid of happiness;
His companions set off for the city,   41

To seek an expert who would
Hold the key to his knotty problem.   42

With hearts afire and eyes brimming,
They raced from street to street.   43

The city that was like a spring garden
Appeared full of thorns to them.   44

From various people they inquired
The secret of that sculpted form.   45

Until in their search, an old man
Offered them the key to a solution.   46

He said, "That figure, fresh as a rose garden,
And tulip-like, grown out of stone,   47

Is the portrait of a beauty of this city,
Whose face no one's eye can enjoy.   48

They have constructed a wooden tower,
Far removed from harm and disturbance.   49

She is in that celestial cradle,
Like a star in the lofty sky.   50

No one is with that heavenly creature
Except for two unmarried slave girls.   51

When the king finds leisure from work,
To relax, he places a ladder at the citadel,   52

Plunders the castle of the beauty there,
And plucks roses from the garden of new spring.   53

He drinks wine and takes his pleasure,
He sleeps, gets up and comes back down.   54

A flower-seller under the king's supervision
Goes to that flowerbed from time to time,   55

She takes roses to the cypress[1] and sits,
While another plucks flowers from the garden.   56

She knows the whole secret of this mystery,
But does not dare speak out.   57

If there is a way to make her acquaintance,
She will be able to shed light on it."   58

As a result of the old man's guidance,
Those young men devised a plan of action.   59

1. The young woman is variously referred to as cypress, moon, rose,
jasmine, idol, etc.

They were resourceful in seeking a solution;
Asking around they found the flower-seller.   60

Secretly they befriended her,
Then sought to solve the problem.   61

According to his means, the merchant's son
Spent his silver like flowing water,   62

Then they went to the flower-seller,
Bearing costly gifts for her.   63

From the friendly gifts,
The flower-seller bloomed like a rose.   64

When they were convinced that secretly
The old woman had become a slave to their generosity,   65

The talented gardener's son set up shop
In the flower-seller's garden.   66

All day he arranged the flowers,
As she sat there watching him.   67

The flower-seller took them to the beauty,
She brought a rose garden before a jasmine.   68

Although his artistry was beyond limit,
For her part she did not reveal the secret.   69

Until one day sensing his opportunity,
He wove a bouquet of many flowers.   70

He wove all kinds of designs
In that beautiful brocade-like bouquet.   71

He gave it to her saying, "Take this splendid gift
There, where you go everyday."   72

The flower-seller took it to the cypress;
She took one rose garden to another.   73

Since that spring of the garden of paradise
Had never seen such a floral creation,   74

The beauty inspected it up and down,
And for a long time remained finger in mouth.[1]   75

Then she said to the old woman, "This fine arrangement
Is not the work of those who made these before.   76

Rather, such precious handiwork is not
The work of any human, let alone you!   77

Who is it that made this floral painting?
What is the secret behind this veil?"   78

The old woman said, "This is my work.
This rose garden is a result of my spring.   79

I create a fitting rose garden out of roses,
Who but I knows how to do this?"   80

The beauty said, "If this is your creation,
Make what you did before in front of me."   81

When the matter came to the test,
The testee was humbled.   82

She said, "Since there is no choice but the truth,
I will disclose the truth from my conscience.   83

A young man is my guest,
He is a stranger away from home.   84

His talent is beyond measure,
and this that you see is the lowliest example of it."   85

Generously the smiling idol poured
Some coins into her lap, saying,   86

___

1. A gesture of astonishment and wonder.

"Since you are his mentor and succor,
Give him these wages for his handiwork." 87

The old woman returned pleased and rejoicing,
And gave the young man the wages for his skill. 88

The gardener's heart bloomed like a rose,
He went and related the event to his friends. 89

When those faithful and well-bred ones
Saw the matter in their grasp, 90

In a private and darkened place
They summoned the old woman. 91

First, they bought her silence with gold,
And then broke the seal from the secret. 92

They narrated the whole story
That was in their afflicted hearts. 93

The heart-rending tale of sorrow,
Of the stone idol and the dejected lover. 94

When the old woman heard the story,
Out of fear her blood turned cold. 95

She said, "Your lips must be sealed!
The heart cannot burn with raw passion. 96

The dome in which the stone idol is,
Is renowned for a thousand leagues. 97

No one sat a moment in that stony edifice
Who was not crushed by that stone. 98

That fair beauty whom no one has seen
Is more stone-hearted than the idol. 99

She has shed the blood of a hundred ardent lovers,
And she has regretted none of it. 100

If anyone in the city utters her name,
They immediately pull out his tongue.   101

It is not prudent to release from confinement
Any word, even by mistake, connected with her."   102

Disappointed those young men
Renewed their acts of kindness.   103

They heaped a treasure by her side,
Even more than the first time.   104

The flower-seller shrank like a violet
At these warm blandishments.   105

She said, "For the sake of half this much,
I will raise a cry in every lane.   106

Your kindness gave me such riches,
That I do not know how to count them.   107

When kindness goes beyond limits,
Then gratitude too knows no boundaries.   108

I will squander my life as a blood price
For the task for which I accept your gift.   109

Whether the matter turns out well or not,
Perforce, I have become one of you.   110

Either I will bring her into our circle
Or I will remove myself from it."   111

The gardener said, "If you are willing,
This request is all that we ask for: 112

Include my handiwork among the flowers
That you take to that tall cypress.   113

Offer my gift to her and whatever she says,
Come back and tell us."   114

The old woman said, "As the matter stands,
What you command is what she desired."   115

At dawn, when flowers bloomed in the garden,
The buds awakened and the narcissus slept,   116

The flower-arranger searched for flowers,
Bunches of them with the scent of musk.   117

With those flowers he fashioned a design:
The form of the idol seen on the wall!   118

He also wove her name into it,
The name befitting the design!   119

Then he blew such a spell upon it
That it made the zephyr lose its control.   120

When the gift reached the grateful lady,
She was again stupefied beyond measure.   121

Seeing her own picture and reading her own name,
She was awed by her own self and her name.   122

By the time she recovered her senses,
Love had cloven her soul into two.   123

A tumult arose in her breast,
And her heart was lost to her.   124

She said gently to the flower-seller,
"All your creations are lovely.   125

What is this flower that has stolen my heart?
And robbed the arrow of prudence from my hand?   126

He who has created this flower arrangement
Has pawned my life to the hands of temptation.   127

Just bring him here once somehow,
So that I may feast my eyes upon him."   128

Striking while the iron was hot,
The old woman applied balm on the wounds.   129

She wove a spell of words and spoke
In bewitching tones to the fairy-like creature,   130

Saying, "You are the sun of lovers!
Kings long for a face such as yours!   131

How is it fitting for a ravishing beauty like you
To utter the name of every beggar?"   132

The delicate beauty's heart knew no rest,
Nothing helped to further the matter.   133

The more evasive the old woman was,
The more she fueled the burning fire;   134

By blowing upon the burning sparks,
She cooked the dish that had to be prepared.   135

Then with firm oaths and promises,
She revealed the secret entirely: 136

The despondency of the companions,
And the stone-worshipping stranger,   137

How a fire arose from that stone in all directions,
Its smoke singeing everything within a hundred leagues,   138

Of the spark from it that fell upon the youth,
As the fire spread here and there.   139

"By a sweet response, you can
Quell the fire with the water of life."   140

The silvery moon replied,
"You who are a trapped deer like me,   141

Many a preying fierce lion
Perishes at my door like a dog.   142

Before I raise the veil of dishonor
From my passionate state of mind,   143

Prepare a subterfuge for this drunkenness,
And perhaps I shall be your accomplice."   144

At this heartening turn of events,
The old woman raced home with dancing feet,   145

Carrying the good news to the friends,
Welcome as rain on a parched field.   146

Each one found renewed joy,
The old hag was made young again.   147

Again they set to work together,
Jointly in seeking a solution.   148

They spoke openly before the old matron,
All that was needed to be discussed,   149

"Of goods and stores and supplies,
of every kind of required skill,   150

We have it all to such an extent,
That every problem will be made easy.   151

But only if our friend is willing and
Is our accomplice in this matter.   152

She should not work against us in trickery,
She should put on the veil rather than remove it."   153

The old woman again hurried off to the lady,
And spoke and heard all that was favorable.   154

When she had forged the bases of a pact,
And calmed the beauty's agitated heart,   155

She returned and poured her heart out,
Saying, "Proceed with whatever is necessary."   156

From the graciousness of the beloved,
The friends blossomed like roses.   157

At night they put their heads together
And deliberated over the details of the plan.   158

Each one again pledged his skill
To the extent of his ability.   159

The gardener said, "Out of camaraderie,
I have displayed all that I know.   160

Whatever else you command me,
I will also do as much as I can."   161

The tunnel-digger said, "We can dig
Secretly under the earth so that   162

We open up a path leading to
That tower rising to the moon."   163

The carpenter turned to the tunnel-digger
And explained what was in his mind,   164

"If your tunnel reaches the tower,
I will enter the tower by a contrivance."   165

The generous merchant said,
"Since our hearts are in accord,   166

It is for you to toil in this matter,
And for me to expend gold and dinars.   167

Let us prepare ourselves for the task
And mint a coin of true friendship.   168

We help our friend attain his desire,
Or we lose our lives and goods."   169

On this agreement and prudent plan,
At night they laid their heads on sleep's pillow.   170

When the sun emerged from its earthly tunnel,
Poking its head out of the celestial portico,   171

The merchant arose resolutely,
And prepared himself for the task.   172

Working with mud and water for some time,
He built a new house in that lane.   173

Its mud was scented with ambergris,
Its yard joyful like the garden of paradise.   174

It had all manner of terraces and porches,
Its arches stretching to the heavens.   175

With scores of rooms and chambers,
No one could fathom its secrets.   176

When the building was tall and complete,
The resolute men set out for their goal.   177

A chamber that was on the inside,
Contained the path of deliverance.   178

The tunnel-digger flexed his muscles
And closing one door, opened the next.   179

He made a path leading to the tower,
Reaching the moon from under the earth.   180

He struck the earth with his steel
In such a way that it lost all control,   181

Until he extended the tunnel
Right to the door of the tower.   182

Then he passed the job on to the carpenter
Who could saw the wood inside.   183

He went into the tunnel right away
To empty the tower with his skill.   184

He put his sharp axe to work and
Splintered the heart of the wood.   185

He worked the wood in a way
That [it] did not seem possible to do.   186

First he opened a door into the tower,
Then turned his skill to the planks.   187

He prepared a ladder, rung by rung,
Leading from inside to the roof of the tunnel.   188

When the skillful man reached the point,
Of opening the secret entrance into the tower,   189

He retreated and emerged from the room,
And informed the old hag of the matter.   190

He said, "Go to the silvery moon,
And see if she is still with us.   191

If she is faithful to her word,
Rid the place of strangers,   192

So that I can open the door to our goal,
Else be silent and return in haste."   193

The old woman left to gauge the mood,
Seeing a favorable moment, she lost her fears.   194

Since the bases of their pact were in place,
And only confidantes were in their chamber,   195

She related the story to the lady
And lifted the veil from the plot.   196

She kicked hard at the entrance
To open the small door of fortune.   197

When the princess looked down into it,
The carpenter emerged greeting her.   198

She responded, "For your expertise,
More than a hundred thousand bravos!   199

For handiwork such as yours,
How can I repay you?   200

If you give me your heart as my guest,
You will enjoy my hospitality.   201

If you prefer to be with your friends,
I myself will come down in due time."   202

The master craftsman answered,
"You of jasmine tresses and sweet words,   203

Although out of your kindness,
You call me your guest,   204

Yet prepare yourself for someone else,
for another is your lover, not I!   205

When you two lovers come together,
I will offer my prayers from afar."   206

So saying he left her presence,
Returning home by way of the opening.   207

The beauty secured the door,
And covered it with some clothes.   208

Then out of longing she dispatched
The old woman to the young man.   209

She handed her a special ring saying,
"Take this greeting to my besotted lover;   210

Tonight I will be awaiting him.
O unseen lover, I am your beloved.   211

If you come as a master to his handmaiden,
I will be the slave of a guest who is dear."   212

Happy the flower-seller blossomed like a flower,
She left and told this story to the friends.   213

One of the friends ran swiftly to the lover,
Carrying the hoped-for good news from his beloved.   214

When he heard the news,
He became even more blissful than before.   215

Stunned by the good turn of events,
His heart's passion spilled into his mind.   216

He leapt up in the manner of smitten lovers,
Who give up their heart's reins to a madman.   217

Stomping his feet in a state of ecstasy,
He entered the secret chamber of union.   218

He imagined a house like the garden of paradise:
With doors, threshold, courts, and harem.   219

First, his friends carried him from his room
And went about making preparations.   220

They bathed him in rosewater and ambergris,
And dressed him in silken robes.   221

Then, from all kinds of tasty items of food,
They offered him bread, sweetmeats, and wine.   222

Meanwhile, the old woman secretly went
And told the lady what she had to tell.   223

The brave and besotted gazelle
Had already deceived the lion,   224

Saying, "I would like to, I must,
Offer prayers within the veil of secrecy.   225

It is better that tonight you stay away,
And excuse me for being far."   226

The simple-minded king believed her,
And left the cypress on her throne.   227

When night allied with the sky,
And the moon sat together with Venus,   228

The princess opened the window of sleep,
So that moonlight could enter inside.   229

She put away the ladder, locked the door,
Opened the secret door and sat waiting.   230

When no more than one watch of the night had passed,
The lion entered the grazing ground of the deer.   231

Two veiled moons emanated light,
Two hearts gave testimony of love.   232

The unseen lovers' hearts became joined,
The two strangers came together.   233

When the lover's soul saw the beloved's face,
It was as if a thirsty man saw the water of life.   234

He took her in his embrace so tightly that
The white poplar sapling turned into a redwood.   235

First he desired a nectar of wine and milk,
Then from her silky body he removed the silk.   236

He imposed a tax of pistachios on sugar,
He put the bodkin in the ivory kohl-container.   237

Through the night until the cock's crowing
The prince's head lay on his bride's tresses.   238

When morning opened the window of light,
Darkness departed from every window.   239

The full moon remained in her abode
And the dragon returned to its lair.   240

The next day when the house was empty
They renewed their pleasure immediately.   241

In this way, when there was leisure from work,
The bazaar of the seditious couple bustled.   242

The prince would enter the moon's window,
And the moon came through the door to the prince.   243

When a few days had passed in this manner,
The two lovers became steadfast in their attachment,   244

The prince said to his friends,
"Bravo to such faithful pals!   245

Each one of you acted so generously that,
All my life, I will not be able to describe it.   246

You have brought the matter to fruition,
Strive so that it does not sour now.   247

Before we tear the veil off,
Let us go and fetch my bride."   248

The merchant said, "Cheer up!
May your enemies lose heart!   249

We are ahead of you in such efforts,
By a pact, we have prepared a veil for the moon.   250

Do not think that we will pack up and leave
This blessed place without the object of desire.   251

It is not fitting nor an exalted thought,
That we obtain the goods by theft.   252

Call us men only at that time,
When we saunter about heroically.   253

We will have a public banquet
And make the moon the king's guest.   254

We will show the treasure to the snake,
And becoming snakes we will rob the treasure."   255

On this accord, they slept happily at night,
And the next day informed the idol of the plan.   256

The beauty said, "Whatever is your order,
I will obey even if my life be in danger."   257

When the plan was fixed with the moon,
The merchant went before the king.   258

He took such manner of presents
That the king remained finger in mouth.   259

He said, "So many gems and treasures
Cannot even be imagined by an appraiser!   260

Why do you present this to me?
Ask what you need to ask for."   261

The merchant said, "May sublime fortune
Be auspicious for the king's crown.   262

In my city I am a merchant;
I am on the road here for myself.   263

Everywhere I went in pursuit of profit,
My gain has been the company of nobles.   264

In every country in which I set foot,
I became acquainted with the ruler of that land,   265

Who upon seeing my regard for guests,
Became *my* guest, obliged to my hand.   266

I am again inclined to that service,
If the gracious king troubles to be my guest."   267

When the king perceived his warmth,
He was embarrassed by the youth's friendliness.   268

He said, "Go and make preparations,
And I will come when you invite me."   269

The host returned again to his home,
And set about putting it in order.   270

He had in his house of pleasure,
Seven floors like the eight paradises.   271

In one he prepared a sumptuous feast,
That distracted Venus's heart from the sky.   272

When night came upon the arrayed company,
The azure heavens took up a goblet.   273

The amiable fellow went forth,
And invited the king to his party.   274

One by one, he got together sweets and wine,
Making his house a wave of pearls on the sea.   275

With one or two boon companions, the king
Came to the party like a swift steed.   276

Night had drawn its veil of darkness;
The wine flowed like the water of life.   277

The sound of tambourines in the ears;
All rendered the chief guest intoxicated.   278

When the bubbling wine made all tipsy,
Every heart was drawn towards beauty.   279

They summoned the moon seated on high
And asked her to cause a sensation.   280

It was arranged that until midnight,
Her form like a wondrous fantasy,   281

A captivating beauty, pleasing to the eyes,
Would strut around with a hundred airs and graces,   282

Just like the moon that appears in the night,
Dressed in black silk from head to toe.   283

Her airs the ruin of the sensible,
Hungry for the blood of lovers,   284

Her beautiful face appeared unveiled,
As the sun in the dark night.   285

By conversing with the revelers
She became the merry *saqi*[1] of the feast.   286

When she took up a goblet in her hand,
All who saw her were slain, not wasted.   287

When the idol came before the king,
First he was lost in her, then in thought.   288

He said, "God! This is that same moon,
Or my heart is blinded and my senses astray.   289

If this is her, how could she dare?
How can a moon descend from the sky?   290

If she is not that moon, it befits her
To be in the arms of a king such as I."   291

At last when his heart knew no rest,
And his mind did not quit its nagging,   292

He summoned and dispatched a companion,
To check on the young cypress.   293

There the man ran like the wind,
And here she stepped into the hole.   294

She entered her palace and changed her garb,
Closing the opening lay down on her bed.   295

1. A cupbearer or wine server.

When the courier arrived in haste,
He saw the moon asleep in private. 296

He returned to bring the news to the king,
Carrying the chamber's secret to the court. 297

Before that the damsel jumped up
And clothed her fair form in black. 298

Goblet in hand, she made the rounds,
Rendering all who saw her senseless. 299

The man who had seen her in her chamber,
Came and informed the king of all he had seen. 300

The king's eye was fixed upon her,
As his mind began to stop its nagging. 301

He was quaffing one drink after another,
Intoxicated by its cupbearer not the wine, 302

Desiring to do what was right,
To free the rose from the garden. 303

That desire was turning in his soul,
Every moment his mouth was watering, 304

Until the moon of the night tossed
The dark veil from her fair face. 305

The king still retained his desire,
He was drunk with a hangover from the *saqi*. 306

He was a young king, in love and intoxicated:
Then how could he have any patience? 307

Although the male lion broke his chains,
He did not lay a paw on his prey. 308

The drunkard rose from his seat,
With a light heart he went home. 309

Here the moon returned to her tower,
Arriving before the king got there. 310

Since Khizr[1] became lost in his own stream,
The stream came to meet him amicably. 311

The coquettish *saqi* whom he sought
Was before him and he searched elsewhere. 312

His beloved was before him and he was pining for her!
His feet were on a treasure and he thought he was
      penniless! 313

The water of life was ebullient in his cup,
As he waited all day for night to come. 314

At night when the moon took up a wine goblet,
And everyone laid their heads to sleep in bed, 315

The previous night's host returned,
And the king's heart became agitated. 316

In anticipation of that sugar-lipped one,
He made his sour expression sweet. 317

The king flattered the youth falsely,
And set off for the feast eagerly. 318

The previous night's feasting was renewed,
The market of pleasure was brisk again. 319

The *saqi* of the night put on a different garb,
And ornamented herself from top to toe. 320

The night was black, her dress the sun,
Tonight her dress was white like Venus. 321

Although that moon was a nocturnal candle,
She showed herself differently to the king. 322

1. The mysterious guide of travelers, especially in seeking the water of life.

When he saw her resplendent beauty,
His mouth was agape in astonishment.   323

The "new" *saqi* robbed his senses such
That he forgot the one from yesterday.   324

He transferred his heart from that one to this,
The garden gave a tulip to the jasmine.   325

He kept his eye on the strutting doll,
His heart he lost, his soul found sight.   326

In this way until dawn,
He begged sweets and wine from that moon.   327

At day, when he hastened home,
He saw his sun fast asleep.   328

He saw that his eyesight had erred,
Last night's moon seemed a dragon.   329

He slept a little and rose like one smitten,
And the beauty also awoke from her slumber.   330

She wrinkled her dainty eyebrows,
And weakened the king by her coquetries.   331

As reproachful he had been,
Now he was a hundred times sorry.   332

She robbed the king in such a manner,
The thief was bold, the watchman stupid.   333

When night hid the visage of the sun,
And the sky created a rose-garden of darkness,   334

The guest went back to the party,
Where the host was friendly,   335

And the *saqi* of the night was all smiles,
Dressed in green like a tall cypress.   336

Again, the king was enraptured by the sight,
A single desire of his heart became a hundred.   337

He said to the one who caused his joy,
"I should be ashamed of my kingship!   338

I, a lord have many beauties at home,
I, a king am obsessed with this form.   339

If I take her by force, it will be unjust,
But otherwise, my patience is at an end."   340

All night until the cock's crowing,
With a thousand regrets he kept drinking.   341

At dawn when he hastened home,
There he found the night's moon.   342

For seven days that idol was decked up,
And the king was deceived time and again.   343

He was busy with his love games,
The young men with their plotting.   344

Not far from that crowded dwelling,
Was the seashore, about a league away,   345

Every preparation for a sea voyage
Was taken care of one by one.   346

When the ship had been equipped,
They went to bid the king farewell.   347

Each one said, "O fortunate king!
My you remain eternally on the exalted throne.   348

We who are the servants of your court,
We beg to be excused of your kindness.   349

As long as we were content in this place,
We were drowned in his lordship's favors.   350

Now that we are ready to depart,
Even our supplies are his lordship's gift.   351

It is wrong to tie up a merchant's capital,
We will profit from the sea for some months.   352

Since the earth's kind bounty
Compels us to leave this city,   353

Whatever we have of goods and riches,
And the dear *saqis* whom the king saw,   354

We will leave back in trust here,
Until God brings us back to this place.   355

It would be well if you keep us in your mind,
And this trust be acceptable to you."   356

When the king heard the mention of the *saqis*,
He became as if he would tear off his clothes.   357

He gave them treasures and made apologies,
He equipped them with all necessities.   358

Then he waited for the chivalrous men
To set off on their journey.   359

He who plunders the treasury
Gains a new city as his booty!   360

His lust overpowered him swiftly,
And he set off like water towards the sea.   361

Beforehand, the conspirators had smuggled
And hidden the bride on the ship.   362

The travelers went to their ship,
Like five angels going to one paradise.   363

There the boat flew like the wind,
And here the king spurred his horse.   364

With a thirsty heart and mouth watering,
He went from the sea to a mirage.   365

He came to the guesthouse,
Lusting for the entrancing fairy.   366

When he entered he saw the house empty,
The sword of his love met with indifference.   367

He ran around the palace and porticoes, rooms and roof,
But the birds had flown the coop.   368

Room after room he searched through,
He poked his head into every window,   369

Until he found his way to the room with the hole
From which the moon used to appear.   370

In the room he noticed something unusual,
A strange opening leading underground.   371

He boldly stepped inside until
The ladder led him to the tower.   372

He entered the tower and it was moonless,
His gall bladder burst from what he saw.   373

With remorse he died in that dashed hope,
She had left and had taken away his wish.   374

Those ones went to their own homes,
Rejoicing in their good fortune.   375

The moon was so happy with her new king
That she did not miss the old one.   376

In all the excitement of the events,
A nagging feeling remained about the flower-seller.   377

They made merry with wine and drink,
But forever grieving for the old flower-seller.   378

She, in memory of her fidelity and succor,
Always wore rose-hued clothes.   379

The Prince and his friends carry off the lady.

CHRONOLOGY

1253 Birth of Amir Khusraw

1266 Balban begins his rule

1272 Becomes Nizamuddin Awliya's disciple

1273 Compiles his first *divan*, *Tuhfat al-sighar*

1280 Accompanies Prince Muhammad to Multan

1284 Compiles his second *divan*, *Vasat al-hayat*

1285 Returns to Delhi

1287 Kayqubad begins his rule

1289 Writes the *Qiran al-sa'dayn*

1290 Jalaluddin Khalji begins his rule

1291 Writes the *Miftah al-futuh*

1294 Compiles his third *divan*, *Ghurrat al-kamal*

1296 'Alauddin Khalji begins his rule

1298 Begins the *khamsah*

1302 Finishes the *khamsah*

1309 Writes the *Khaza'in al-futuh*

1310 Compiles the *I'jaz-i Khusravi*

1315 Writes the *Duval Rani Khizr Khan*

1316 Compiles his fourth *divan*, *Baqiyah naqiyah*; Mubarak Shah begins his rule

1318 Writes the *Nuh sipihr*

1320 Usurpation of Khusraw Khan; Ghiyasuddin Tughlaq begins his rule; writes the *Tughlaqnamah*

1325 Muhammad Shah Tughlaq begins his rule; death of Nizamuddin Awliya and Amir Khusraw; the fifth *divan*, *Nihayat al-jamal*, is compiled

GLOSSARY

basant South Asian spring festival celebrated by the Chishti sufis

dargah Tomb of a sufi which is visited by devotees, where *qawwali* is performed and *'urs* takes place

divan Collection of a poet's lyric and panegyric works

ghazal Love lyric that is sung in either a secular or mystical setting

ghazi Warrior for the cause of Islam

iham *Double entendre* or pun

jama'atkhanah see *khanaqah*

khamsah Quintet of narrative poems in the *masnavi* form

khanaqah Sufi establishment headed by a *pir* where mystical gatherings take place

malfuzat Sayings and discourses of a sufi *pir* as recorded by one of his disciples

masnavi Narrative poem with a heroic, didactic/sufi, or romantic theme, in rhymed couplets

muezzin One who gives the call to prayer from a mosque

nadim Boon companion to a king or prince

pir Elder or sufi master, also known as *murshid*

qasidah Ceremonious panegyric poem in honor of a patron

qawwal One who performs *qawwali*

qawwali Ecstatic and hypnotic performance of sufi verses, sometimes accompanied by dance

qiblah Direction of Mecca, which Muslims face for prayer

sama' Audition of music by sufis to induce spiritual ecstasy

saqi Cupbearer or wine server at royal banquets, usually a young boy

silsilah Sufi order whose leadership is passed from one *pir* to another

'urs Celebration of a symbolic marriage with God that signifies the death anniversary of a mystic

BIBLIOGRAPHY

WORKS OF AMIR KHUSRAW

Divans

Dībāchah-yi Dīvān-i Ghurrat al-Kamāl. Ed. Sayyid Vazīr al-Hasan
 'Ābidī. Islamabad: Naishnal Kamītī barā'e Sātsau Sālah Taqrībāt-i
 Amīr Khusrau, 1975.
Dīvān-i kāmil-i Amīr Khusraw. Ed. Said Nafisi, Mahmud Darvish.
 Tehran: Jāvīdān, 1982.
Kullīyāt-i Amīr Khusraw. Ed. Anvar al-Hasan. Lucknow: Naval Kishor,
 1967.
Kullīyāt-i ghazalīyāt-i Khusraw. Ed. Iqbal Salahuddin. Lahore:
 Paykijaz, 1972.
Kullīyāt-i qasā'id-i Khusraw. Ed. Iqbal Salahuddin. Lahore: National
 Book Foundation, 1977.

Khamsah

Ā'īnah-i Iskandarī. Ed. J. Mirsayyidov. Moscow: Khāvar, 1977.
Hasht bihisht. Ed. J. Iftikhar. Moscow: Khāvar, 1972.
Khamsah. Tehran: Shaqāyiq, 1983. (Reprint of the Moscow
 editions)
Le otto novelle del paradise. Tr. Angelo M. Piemontese. Roma: Salerno,
 2000. (Italian translation)
Lo specchio Alessandrino. Tr. Angelo M. Piemontese. Soveria Mannelli
 (Catanzaro): Rubbettino, 1999. (Italian translation)
Majnūn va Laylā. Ed. T. A. Muharramov. Moscow: Khāvar, 1964.
Matla' al-anvār. Ed. T. A. Muharramov. Moscow: Khāvar, 1975.
Shīrīn va Khusraw. Ed. Gh. Aliev. Moscow: Khāvar, 1961.

Historical poems

Duval Rānī Khizr Khān. Ed. Khaliq Ahmad Nizami. Delhi: Idārah-i
Adabīyāt-i Dillī, 1988.
Masnavī-yi Nuh sipihr. Ed. Mohammad Wahid Mirza. London:
Oxford University Press, 1950.
Masnavī-yi Nuh sipihr. Tr. Muhammad Rafīq ʿĀbid. New Delhi:
Maktabah Jāmiʿah, 1979. (Urdu translation)
Masnavī-yi Tughlaqnāmah-i Khusraw Dihlavī. Ed. Sayyid Hāshimī
Farīdābādī. Hyderabad: Majlis-i Makhtūtāt-i Fārsī,
1932.
Miftāh al-futūh. Ed. Shaikh Abdur Rashid. Aligarh: Department of
History, Aligarh Muslim University, 1954.
Qirān al-saʿdayn. Ed. Ahmad Hasan Qari. Islamabad: Markaz-i
Tahqīqāt-i Īrān va Pākistān, 1976.
Zamīmah-i Tughlaqnāmah-i Amīr Khusraw. Ed. S.A.H. Abidi and
S. Maqbul Ahmad. Dihlī: Indo-Parshiyan Sosāʾitī, 1975.

Prose

*The Campaigns of ʿAlāʾuʾd-dīn Khiljī, being the Khazāʾinul Futūh
(Treasures of Victory)*. Tr. Muhammad Habib. Bombay: D.B.
Taraporewala, Sons & Co., 1931. (English translation)
Iʿjāz-i Khusravī. Lucknow: Naval Kishor, 1876.
Khazāʾin al-futūh. Ed. M. Wahid Mirza. Calcutta: Asiatic Society,
1953.

SECONDARY SOURCES

Abdurrahman, Sabahuddin. *Amir Khusrau as a Genius*. Delhi: Idārah-i
Adabiyāt-i Dillī, 1982.
Amir Khusrau: Critical Studies. Islamabad: National Committee for
700th Anniversary of Amir Khusrau, 1975.
Amir Khusrau: Memorial Volume. New Delhi: Publications Division,

Government of India, Ministry of Information and Broadcasting, 1975.

Ansari, Zoe, ed. *Life, Times & Works of Amīr Khusrau Dehlavī*. New Delhi: National Amir Khusrau Society, 1975.

Azad, Muhammad Husain. *Ab-e hayāt: Shaping the Canon of Urdu Poetry*. Tr. & ed., Frances Pritchett, Shamsur Rahman Faruqi. New Delhi: Oxford University Press, 2001.

Brend, Barbara. *Perspectives of Persian Painting: Illustrations to Amir Khusrau's Khamsah*. London: RoutledgeCurzon, 2003.

de Bruijn, J.T.P. *Persian Sufi Poetry: An Introduction to the Mystical Use of Classical Persian Poems*. Richmond: Curzon, 1997.

Ernst, Carl W. and Bruce B. Lawrence. *Sufi Martyrs of Love: The Chishti Order in South Asia and Beyond*. New York: Palgrave Macmillan, 2002.

Habib, Mohammad. *Hazrat Amir Khusrau of Delhi*. Bombay: Taraporevala Sons and Co., 1927. (Reprint; Lahore, 1979).

Hasan Nizami. *Taj ul ma'athir (The crown of glorious deeds)*. Tr. Bhagwat Saroop. Delhi: Saud Ahmad Dehlavi, 1998.

Hasan Sijzi. *Nizam Ad-Din Awliya: Morals for the Heart*. Tr. Bruce B. Lawrence. New York: Paulist Press, 1992.

Husain, Mumtaz. *Amir Khusrav Dehlavi*. Karachi: Saad Publications, 1986.

Amīr Khusrau: hayāt aur shā'irī. Islamabad: Naishnal Kamītī barā'e Sātsau Sālah Taqrībāt-i Amīr Khusrau, 1975.

Ibn Battuta. *Travels in Asia and Africa, 1325–1354*. Tr. H.A.R. Gibb. London: Routledge & Kegan Paul, 1957.

Jackson, Peter. *The Delhi Sultanate: A Political and Military History*. Cambridge: Cambridge University Press, 1999.

Kidwai, Saleem and Ruth Vanita. *Same-Sex Love in India: Readings from Literature and History*. New York: Palgrave, 2000.

Lewis, Franklin D. *Rumi: Past and Present, East and West*. Oxford: Oneworld, 2000.

Meisami, Julie S. *Medieval Persian Court Poetry*. Princeton: Princeton University Press, 1987.

Meraj Ahmed Nizami. *Surūd-e rūhānī: qavvālī ke rang.* Delhi: Ghulam
   Hasnain, 1998.

Mirza, Mohammad Wahid. *Life and Works of Amir Khusrau.* Lahore:
   Panjab University Press, 1962. (Reprint; Delhi, 1974).

Nath, R. and Faiyaz Gwaliari. *India as Seen by Amir Khusrau (in
   1318 A.D.).* Jaipur: Historical Research Documentation
   Programme, 1981.

Qureshi, Regula Burckhardt. *Sufi Music of India and Pakistan: Sound,
   Context, and Meaning in Qawwali.* Chicago: University of Chicago
   Press, 1995.

Renard, John, ed. *Windows on the House of Islam: Muslim Sources on
   Spirituality and Religious Life.* Berkeley: University of California
   Press, 1998.

Samnani, S. Ghulam. *Amir Khusrau.* New Delhi: National Book
   Trust, 1968.

Seyller, John. *Pearls of the Parrot of India: The Walters Art Museum
   Khamsa of Amīr Khusraw of Delhi.* Baltimore: Walters Art
   Museum, 2001.

INDEX

MAKERS *of the* MUSLIM WORLD

Series Editor: Patricia Crone
Institute for Advanced Study, Princeton

Among the over fifty titles in the series:

Ibn 'Arabi
William C. Chittick
Renowned expert William Chittick
surveys the life and works of this
legendary thinker.
ISBN: 1-85168-387-9

Shaykh Mufid
T. Bayhom-Daou
An assessment of the great Shi'ite
scholar and theologian.
ISBN: 1-85168-383-6

Abu Nuwas
Philip Kennedy
A readable introduction to this
celebrated 9th-century poet.
ISBN: 1-85168-360-7

'Abd al-Malik
Chase F. Robinson
The Umayyad Caliph and founder
of the Dome of the Rock is
captured in a concise and
clear manner.
ISBN: 1-85168-361-5

Fazlallah Astarabadi
and the Hurufis
Shahzad Bashir
Discusses the achievements of this
Sufi thinker and founder of Gnostic
Hurufism.
ISBN: 1-85168-385-2

al-Ma'mun
Michael Cooperson
An introduction to the controversial
9th-century Caliph and patron of the
sciences.
ISBN: 1-85168-386-0

Ahmad Riza Khan
Usha Sanyal
On the founder of the 'Barelwi' move-
ment in India in the late 19th/early
20th centuries.
ISBN: 1-85168-359-3

Amir Khusraw
Sunil Sharma
Surveys the life and work of the 14th-
century Indian poet, courtier, musician,
and Sufi.
ISBN: 1-85168-362-3

'Abd al-Rahman III
Maribel Fierro
Introduces the founder of the great
Caliphate of Madinat al-Zahra at
Cordova.
ISBN: 1-85168-384-4

el-Hajj Beshir Agha
Jane Hathaway
An examination of the longest serving
Chief Harem Eunuch in the history of
the Ottoman Empire.
ISBN: 1-85168-390-9

www.oneworld-publications.com